REGIS COLLEGE LIBRARY

◁ SO-AYH-560

"The ministers who wrote these chapters are intent on building intercultural communities that embody new forms of church and society. Sharing a common faith does not guarantee anything about common life, common worship, or common action. But with the creative, concerted, compassionate efforts reported here, we discover new ways to advance that work. This is a compelling resource for forward-looking congregations and students of ministry."

—Mary E. Hunt, Co-director,
Women's Alliance for Theology, Ethics, and Ritual (WATER)

"Buried deep in the subterranean recesses of this thoughtful, provoking, timely collection of essays representing the breadth of world Christianity is the fundamental, and ultimately transformative, not to mention far-reaching insight, that diversity, multiculturalism, inclusion, in and for theological education and ministry, are not enough. Their futures, and indeed the future of our planet, depend on the creation and nurture of intercultural competencies that are not only practical, but learned; critical but also hopeful; uncompromising, while being gracious; strategic, and at the same time tactical.

"This is a volume that will not only disturb but also comfort, disrupt as well as protect, both the faithful and the cynical, providing readers with 'solid' resources and 'liquid' perspectives for ministry and the living out of their lives—especially in these deeply troubled and troubling times.

"*Intercultural Ministry* is a must-read for all peoples of goodwill who desire the 'creation of the fundamentally new that is also fundamentally better' as they aspire to repair our broken world."

—Lester Edwin J. Ruiz, MDiv, PhD, Senior Director,
Accreditation and Institutional Evaluation,
The Association of Theological Schools,
The Commission on Accrediting

REGIS COLLEGE LIBRARY
100 Wellesley Street West
Toronto, Ontario
Canada M5S 2Z5

"This impressive collection of essays gathers years of wisdom from seasoned pastoral leaders. By combining personal narrative, theological reflection on current events, and practical suggestions for the church, the authors offer abundant resources for pastors, scholars, and students engaged in the work of intercultural ministry. They do not sugarcoat the many challenges of this work in our time, but they do offer the outlines of hope for a more intercultural future."

—David H. Jensen, Academic Dean and
Professor in the Clarence N. and Betty B. Freierson
Distinguished Chair of Reformed Theology,
Austin Presbyterian Theological Seminary

"In pulling together the fifteen essays that make up *Intercultural Ministry: Hope for a Changing World*, editors Grace Ji-Sun Kim and Jann Aldredge-Clanton have done a great service to congregational leaders seeking a faithful way forward in the midst of one of the defining challenges of our time—the fact that in a world of ever-increasing mixing of races, ethnicities, and nationalities, the vast majority of churches remain stubbornly segregated. Acknowledging that creating intercultural communities is often a 'disorienting, shocking, and at times, traumatic' process that never occurs without conflict and never comes to completion, the authors clear away naïveté and dismiss simplistic answers, offering instead a vision that is honest, complex, and nuanced enough to actually be helpful. Even while addressing the difficulties, the authors testify to the transformative power of such communities and offer a stirring reminder that these churches continue a story that began with Christianity's first congregations, the power necessary to create them being inherent in our faith itself and the Spirit that gave it birth."

—Rev. LeDayne McLeese Polaski, Executive Director/Directora
Ejecutiva, BPFNA ~ Bautistas por la Paz

"Grace Ji-Sun Kim and Jann Aldredge-Clanton have done a phenomenal work as they gathered essays from a diverse group of religious leaders to discuss the creation and implementation of intercultural ministry in their communities. A copy of this masterpiece should be in every theologian's library as a reference book which gives understanding to the importance of intercultural ministries as we attempt to live in our diverse communities that are constantly changing."

—Rev. Leslie Robin Harrison, Itinerant Elder
of the African Methodist Episcopal Church

"For those committed to reflecting God's diverse future today, *Intercultural Ministry* is an invaluable tool. What passes for multicultural church is often a surface mix of people of different races and ethnicities, but they essentially share the same culture. This book challenges us to go deeper—too deep perhaps for some!—as it provides the theological and practical resources to move the church toward genuine interculturalism. It calls for openness on our part to the Spirit's work to change the heart and soul of the church, and not just its face."

— Al Tizon, Executive Minister of Serve Globally,
Evangelical Covenant Church,
and author of *Missional Preaching*

"Creating and sustaining a ministry that embraces diversity within the leadership and the membership has been the great challenge of the church from its inception. This book is a much needed guideline on how to overcome those barriers."

—Marvin A. McMickle, PhD, President and
Professor of Church Leadership,
Colgate Rochester Crozer Divinity School

Intercultural Ministry

HOPE FOR A CHANGING WORLD

GRACE JI-SUN KIM | JANN ALDREDGE-CLANTON
EDITORS

Foreword by Dwight N. Hopkins

REGIS COLLEGE LIBRARY
100 Wellesley Street West
Toronto, Ontario
Canada M5S 2Z5

BV
4400
I58
2017

JUDSON PRESS
PUBLISHERS SINCE 1824

Join our mailing list for updates and special offers.
www.judsonpress.com/mailing_list.cfm

Intercultural Ministry: Hope for a Changing World
© 2017 by Judson Press, Valley Forge, PA 19482-0851
All rights reserved.

No part of this publication may be reproduced, stored in a retrieval system, or transmitted in any form or by any means, electronic, mechanical, photocopying, recording, or otherwise, without the prior permission of the copyright owner, except for brief quotations included in a review of the book.

Judson Press has made every effort to trace the ownership of all quotes. In the event of a question arising from the use of a quote, we regret any error made and will be pleased to make the necessary correction in future printings and editions of this book.

Bible quotations in this volume are from the Common English Bible © 2011 Common English Bible. Used by permission. All rights reserved. Holy Bible, New International Version®, NIV® Copyright ©1973, 1978, 1984, 2011 by Biblica, Inc.® Used by permission. All rights reserved worldwide. New King James Version. Copyright © 1972, 1984 by Thomas Nelson Inc. New Revised Standard Version Bible, copyright © 1989, Division of Christian Education of the National Council of the Churches of Christ in the United States of America. Used by permission. All rights reserved. Revised Standard Version of the Bible, copyright © 1946, 1952, 1971 by the Division of Christian Education of the National Council of the Churches of Christ in the U.S.A. Used by permission.

Interior design by Wendy Ronga / Hampton Design Group.
Cover design by Lisa Delgado and Delgado & Associates.

Library of Congress Cataloging-in-Publication Data
Names: Kim, Grace Ji-Sun, 1969- editor.
Title: Intercultural ministry: hope for a changing world / edited by Grace Ji-Sun Kim & Jann Aldredge-Clanton; foreword by Dwight N. Hopkins. Description: first [edition]. | Valley Forge: Judson Press, 2017. Identifiers: LCCN 2016031976 (print) | LCCN 2016040671 (ebook) | ISBN 9780817017798 (pbk. : alk. paper) | ISBN 9780817081690 (e-book) Subjects: LCSH: Church work. | Cultural pluralism—Religious aspects—Christianity. | Pastoral theology. Classification: LCC BV4400 .I47 2017 (print) | LCC BV4400 (ebook) | DDC 253.089—dc23
LC record available at https://lccn.loc.gov/2016031976

Printed in the U.S.A.
First printing, 2017.

To Rev. Sukhyon Peter Han, who guided me and paved the way for my interest in intercultural ministry. —Grace

In loving memory of my mother, Eva Aldredge Henley, who engaged in intercultural ministry before it was defined. —Jann

Contents

REGIS COLLEGE LIBRARY
100 Wellesley Street West
Toronto, Ontario
Canada M5S 2Z5

REGIS COLLEGE LIBRARY
100 Wellesley Street West
Toronto, Ontario
Canada M5S 2Z5

Foreword

Amid the proliferation of today's chatter over the United States being part of a global village, it is refreshing to receive a book steeped in scholarship with a compassion that knows that everyday people's lives matter. Grace Ji-Sun Kim and Jann Aldredge-Clanton are the first to achieve this major feat with *Intercultural Ministry: Hope for a Changing World*.

They offer a marvelous opportunity for Christians and other empathetic people to move beyond diversity and work toward intercultural ministry. Diversity, indeed, can represent a phase in building better connections among people. But how do we build healthy communities that bring us together as next-door neighbors and global neighbors? We each cherish our family heritages and values, of course. Our own locations give us meaning and human specificity. Yet, we know that pollution in any part of the country reverberates across the land. Weather patterns disrupted now redesign seasonal swings in other regions. Airborne viruses can jump on a plane and soon travel from the East to the West Coast. A technological innovation of a smartphone application in a little garage in the South has the potential to save lives in the North.

And then, there was One who traveled the byways of Palestine about two thousand years ago. Jesus called on families from all walks of life to celebrate who they were while extending a hand to the villagers nearby. This life of Jesus and the best of Christian legacies compel us to enter into a way of life of intercultural engagement—the interaction of people across races, ethnicities, and nationalities to learn to value and celebrate each group's traditions. Likewise, our increasing communications immediacies move us beyond diversity and into explorations between cultures.

It is long overdue for churches to prepare themselves for what might be the defining theological line of the twenty-first century—how to be curious about, have sympathy for, and develop long-term friendships in the mixing of the world's cultures.

Just imagine in an eight-hour period, first video conferencing East Asia in the morning on one's smartphone, then the same for Ghana, followed by a laptop visual discussion with Cyprus, and finishing off the evening with a simultaneous five-country visual conversation with other friends. Imagine every Wednesday morning, Christians from four different regions of the world having prayer on the phone together. And for us citizens of the USA, it is not just about intercultural dynamics for Christianity and ministries "out there." More and more, we are encountering our new neighbors in our churches, our ministries, our divinity schools, seminaries, and schools of religions. People from Africa, Asia, the Caribbean, the Pacific Islands, South America, and the former Soviet Union states appear routinely in our student bodies, on our faculties, on our staffs, and as financial contributors to our religious institutions.

The ongoing modern democratic experiment that is the United States, with all of its mixing and matching of differences, with all of its scars and absurdities requiring prophetic ministries, still can present to the international community a form of Christianity as hope for healthy communities. By this I mean that the United States of North America is the one country with citizens descended from every other country. And that has the potential to be a pathway paradigm for friends and neighbors globally. Yet, simultaneously, the possibility can be birthed only when citizens of the United States grasp and commit forever to the world's cultures. Isn't that what the gospel proclaims? "God so loved the world . . ."

—Dwight N. Hopkins, PhD, PhD
Professor of Theology, University of Chicago Divinity School

Acknowledgments

Books arise from dialogue and from need. This book did just that. We felt an urgent need to heal divisions by bringing people together across races and cultures to give equal value and power to each one. There is a great need for churches to claim our prophetic calling to make the gospel vision of radically inclusive love and justice a reality. Now more than ever, our world needs intercultural churches and ministries as they contribute to understanding, justice, peacemaking, equality, mutuality, freedom, and respect.

With the desire to help meet these needs, we began this book project. We want to thank many people who helped us make our vision for this book a reality. We thank Rev. Rebecca Irwin-Diehl, Lisa Blair, and other staff at Judson Press who recognized the importance of our book project. They were excited about our project right from the start and helped us each step of the way.

We thank Dr. Dwight Hopkins for his generous Foreword. We also thank each of our contributors. They spent a great deal of time reflecting and writing about intercultural ministry. Their thoughtfulness, kindness, and vision of intercultural ministry are woven into this book. For their dedication and for their ministries, we are grateful.

Our institutions have been supportive of our writing. Grace thanks Earlham School of Religion (ESR) for being so encouraging and interested in all of her work, inside the classroom and outside the classroom. ESR puts a lot of emphasis on ministry and how we can welcome those who are different from us. This has been good for her ongoing writing projects. In particular, Grace thanks her dean, Dr. Jay Marshall, and her colleagues at ESR who challenge her and are genuinely interested in her work.

Jann thanks colleagues at Perkins School of Theology and Richland College who have supported her work. She also thanks Equity for Women in the Church Community, especially her cochair Sheila Sholes-Ross, for living the vision of intercultural ministry, for enthusiastic support of this project, and for contributing to the book. Jann also thanks Colette Casburn Numajiri, one of the ministers in New Wineskins Feminist Ritual Community, for her encouragement and contributions to this project. Colette went with Jann on the adventure of visiting numerous churches in the Dallas area, trying to find intercultural congregations.

Grace is also grateful to her family for their unconditional support in publishing her book. She is thankful to her sister, Karen, and brother-in-law, Bruce, for their support. Her niece, Naomi, and nephew, Matthew, have always shown keen interest in her writing and ministry. Her three children, Theo, Elisabeth, and Joshua, are busy engaged in youth group and other church activities. Their interests in church and church ministry have always been a good resource for Grace. She also thanks her husband, Perry, who has done more than is expected so that she can finish this book. To family and friends, she is forever thankful and grateful.

Jann is indeed thankful to her family for their strong support of this book project and all her work. Her husband, David, two sons, Chad and Brett, and daughter-in-law, Beth, continually give encouragement and good ideas for her work. Through their important work in church and society, they contribute to understanding, justice, equality, and love in the world. She thanks her grandsons, Lyle, Emmett, and Paul, for also bringing her joy and love. For their inspiration and celebration of her work, Jann is also grateful to her many friends in New Wineskins Feminist Ritual Community, Christian Feminism Today, Equity for Women in the Church Community, Alliance of Baptists, and Church in the Cliff.

Introduction

Rev. Dr. Grace Ji-Sun Kim and
Rev. Dr. Jann Aldredge-Clanton

Martin Luther King Jr. often repeated this indictment in his preaching and teaching: "Sunday at 11:00 a.m. is the most segregated hour in America." More than fifty years later, Sunday morning continues to be one of the most segregated times. While the number of racially segregated churches is decreasing, about 86 percent "of American congregations (containing 80 percent of religious service attendees) remain overwhelmingly white or black or Hispanic or Asian or whatever."[1]

Why are most churches still segregated by race and culture? Is it possible to build intercultural churches and ministries today? What are the challenges of creating and maintaining these ministries? How do intercultural churches give equal power and privilege to each culture? How do they avoid assimilating minority cultures into dominant cultures? Are intercultural churches desirable? Will they help eliminate racially motivated hate crimes? Will they advance racial equality and justice?

Intercultural Ministry: Hope for a Changing World explores these questions and more. We have invited pastors, theologians, and teachers to write chapters with their reflections on intercultural churches and ministry.

We use the word *intercultural* to include "interracial," but in a wider sense of including nationalities and ethnicities as well as races. By "intercultural" we mean the interaction of people across races, ethnicities, and nationalities to learn to value and celebrate each group's traditions.

We believe that intercultural churches and ministries move beyond diversity. Many churches welcome people of various races and even take pride in the diversity of their membership, pointing to a scattering of people from races other than the dominant race. Other churches claim diversity because they have a Hispanic congregation, an African congregation, and an Asian congregation meeting in the same building with the dominant white congregation. Others point to the diversity in their surrounding community. For example, on one street in Dallas, Texas, there is a Vietnamese church, an Eritrean church, and an Ethiopian church.

People within diverse churches and congregations of different cultures may exist side by side, but they do not come together to learn from one another and to engage one another in mutual relationships. They do nothing to change the power imbalances that persist when one culture remains dominant. They may be diverse, but they are not intercultural.

Intercultural churches and ministries bring people of various cultures together to learn from one another, giving equal value and power to each culture, preserving cultural differences, and celebrating the variety of cultural traditions. Intercultural churches and ministries are defined by justice, mutuality, respect, equality, understanding, acceptance, freedom, peacemaking, and celebration. In intercultural churches people must be willing to leave the comfort zones of their own separate traditions. For example, they cannot cling to high church worship, often associated with white congregations, or to more celebratory styles, often associated with African American congregations. They must be willing to embrace different styles of worship. As people from different cultures interact with one another and build relationships, they grow together and become transformed.

We have felt called to explore the facets of intercultural ministry in this book because for many years we have believed in the transforming possibilities of intercultural churches and have tried to live out this belief through our varied ministry experiences.

Grace's Experience

I grew up in a Korean Presbyterian church in London, Ontario, in Canada. It was a very conservative church that did not allow women's leadership or women pastors. It was a constricting church experience because I felt limited as a Christian to live out my faith fully and powerfully.

Growing up as a child of an immigrant family was not always easy. It was difficult to grow up in a small city where the majority of the population was white. My father wanted my sister and me to experience some of the white cultural and religious aspects of our small city. Since my father wanted us to be exposed to other denominations and non-Korean churches, we spent a lot of time at a Baptist church, attending Sunday night services and Wednesday night Bible studies. In addition, on Friday nights, we went to the Missionary Alliance church for Bible study and fellowship. Thus I grew up in a mix of denominational church settings and in racially diverse churches. These experiences in various intercultural church settings have informed my own vocation as a Korean American woman.

Growing up in a Korean Presbyterian church, I saw how my Korean church experiences were marginalized in ecumenical circles and in the church universal. The problems that I faced in society due to my ethnicity and gender I also faced in the wider church. The white church tended to look down on Korean American churches. Many of the pastors and leaders were not fluent English speakers, nor did they understand the white dominant culture well. So we were often viewed as lesser than. It was difficult to grow up on the margins of society as well as on the margins of the church.

From this personal experience I have come to recognize how important it is to the wider church to make Sunday mornings as inclusive as possible. The inclusivity comes not only in ethnicity but also in culture, class, gender, sexuality, ability, and education.

Canada is a multinational country with a diversity of people from various backgrounds. In contrast to the assimilationist "melting pot" image frequently associated with the United States,[2] Canada is a pluralistic "mosaic." As a cultural mosaic, Canada encompasses many cultures, religions, and ideas that coexist with one another.

Multiculturalism understands that the world cannot be universally defined. However, multiculturalism is inadequate because it retains an assumption of white culture as normative.[3] Racism occurs in various forms, and it is often institutionalized.

For a society, and a church, to be welcoming of all cultures, its members must be able to rejoice in and live with differences. It is important to incorporate a different approach to religious, theological, or church understanding that accepts and welcomes all races and cultures. Homi Bhabha, professor of humanities at Harvard University, claimed that multiculturalism is a form of exoticism. As such, it creates an ethnic essentialism, where purity of cultural practices must be maintained and supported in order for that culture to be recognized as authentic.[4] It is impossible to keep a culture pure, as there are many forces—external and internal—that cause it to adapt itself, modify, and metamorphasize.

Thus what the church needs is not a multicultural ministry but rather an intercultural community. In an intercultural community, there is a "comprehensive mutuality, reciprocity, and equality."[5] It seeks to build just, mutual, respecting, equal, accepting, and diverse communities. Such a community cultivates a mutual and reciprocal relationship among cultures, which effects transformation in one another.[6]

In a world that is becoming more and more global, we need to recognize the importance of intercultural church, theology, and ministries. As people continue to immigrate and live as neighbors with other cultures, it is getting increasingly crucial that intercultural societies and churches emerge. This will help us work toward building better and warmer relationships between racialized people and the dominant society. The more interracial and intercultural a congregation can become, the more possibility there is of building the reign of God here on earth. Intercultural church ministry is a welcomed possibility for many people who desire varied ways of worshiping when God's people of all backgrounds are able to praise, study, and fellowship together under one roof.

As I finished seminary and was starting my PhD program in theology at the University of St. Michael's College in Toronto, I recognized the need to branch out of my Korean American church and engage in ministry that is moving toward an intercultural church. Thus, I decided to take the position of children's ministry at Celebration Church, which is predominantly Asian, including Chinese, Taiwanese, Korean, and also white.

The varied cultures make worship services and Bible studies interesting, provoking, and challenging. During my time of ministry at Celebration Church, I came to understand that the church universal is a bigger body than just Korean Canadians or Korean Americans. The church is bigger than any one ethnic group. It needs to be inclusive of everybody. It needs to challenge the body of Christ to grow, engage, and multiply.

Jann's Experience

Soon after I was ordained in 1985, many years before I had heard the terms "white privilege" and "intersectionality," I understood on some level that sexism and racism are connected. When asked by a local newspaper about my New Year's resolutions, I said I wanted to help eliminate sexism and racism. In my naïve idealism I had no idea how difficult it might be to keep this resolution. But I soon learned. I would also come to see that racism, sexism, heterosexism, classism, and all injustices are connected and to understand that while I experienced sexism, especially as an ordained

Baptist woman minister, I also experienced privilege as white, straight, and middle-class.

As a minister in Waco, Texas, from 1985 to 1992, I joined a small group of African Americans and whites to form a worship community committed to gender and racial inclusiveness. We wanted to provide an alternative to patriarchal segregated churches. To make our mission clear, we began by calling ourselves the "Alternative Worship Community: intentionally integrated, deliberately inclusive in language, and open to all people." Soon we dropped this unwieldy title and became the "Inclusive Worship Community." To fulfill our egalitarian mission, we had no paid leaders but gave equal value to the gifts of all members, who rotated leadership responsibilities. We did not build or rent worship space but accepted the hospitality of several churches. For about a year we met at a predominantly white Presbyterian church, and then moved to a predominantly black African Methodist Episcopal church. We hoped that this move would increase participation of African Americans in the Inclusive Worship Community, but only a few more African Americans came.

In our idealism we thought that people who suffered from racism would come together with people who suffered from sexism to work on common goals of equal opportunity. But we discovered the truth of womanist theologian Monica A. Coleman's words: "Some churches can see race all day long and not see gender, and vice versa, which I just don't get; it's all the same stuff!"[7] The founders of the Inclusive Worship Community saw this connection between racial and gender justice, but some who came to our worship services did not. At times when African Americans led the services, they did not include women in leadership and the language was exclusively masculine. At times when white women led the services, they did not include people of color.

One of our greatest challenges was keeping our commitment to inclusive language and symbolism. Many of us in the Inclusive Worship Community had come to realize that both inclusive leadership and inclusive sacred symbolism are vital to racial and gender equality. We had written and preached to persuade people of the importance of including biblical female names of God and racially diverse images of God in worship. Many people joined the Inclusive Worship Community because this was the only faith community where they could find inclusive language and symbolism. But others resisted changing traditional exclusively white male imagery for God. One of the African American founders of the community, when she invited black females and males to the community, had trouble convincing them that inclusive sacred symbolism is a justice issue. Many dismissed it as a white middle-class women's issue.

Listening to one another's stories brought deeper respect for differences, while building bridges. A black male minister identified with our struggle to include female divine imagery because of the difficulty he was having trying to persuade his predominantly black church to change from white to black pictures of Christ. It seems ironic that many African Americans want only white sacred symbols, just as so many women cling to male symbols. This minister had discovered the importance of black images of Deity through the study of black liberation theology. As he heard the stories of women, he came to understand the need also for female divine images. Just as black images of God helped him feel that he is truly created in the divine image, he could see that female images of God would help women claim the divine image.

He went deeper to realize the value of female divine images not only for women but also for himself, when one of the members of the community told a compelling story of a rape victim's vision of Christ as a raped woman. He shared his feelings of identification with this image of Christ, lamenting the rape of the entire African American race. "He went on to identify with the psychological dynamics of raped women. Like these women, he had gone through denial for the sake of survival and then the anger that comes with recognition of the violence."[8]

Although the Inclusive Worship Community continued to face challenges, we experienced transformation as we shared our stories, developed mutual relationships, and learned from our varied cultures.

During this time I also attempted to start a church with an African American male as co-pastor. The terms "white privilege" and "male privilege" were not commonly used at the time, but I believed that a white woman and a black man could somehow be equal in privilege, and that by serving as co-pastors we could model racial and gender equality for the church. I understood that churches would not be racially integrated unless the leaders include more than one race and that there could be no gender equality unless women served as equals to men as leaders. My conversations with the male minister about starting a new church moved along with enthusiasm and respect. But he kept saying that he would be glad for me to assist him in various ministries, and I soon realized that he could envision me as his assistant pastor but not as co-pastor.

Years later my vision of co-pastoring with an African American minister has become a reality. My co-pastor is an African American woman, Rev. Sheila Sholes-Ross. We co-pastor a community working for gender and racial equality in churches: Equity for Women in the Church, an intercultural, ecumenical organization with the mission of facilitating equal representation of clergy-women as pastors of intercultural churches in order to transform church and society.

At the time Sheila and I began our work together, I had come to understand my white privilege more fully and to label it as such. Although we share a lack of privilege because of our gender, I know that I have a level of privilege as a white woman that Sheila does not have. From the beginning we committed to transparent conversations about my privilege and to ensuring that we work as equals and that the whole community sees us as equal leaders. We understand that by coming together as a black woman and a white woman to serve as equal leaders, we model racial equality.

We held a national conference to develop strategies for accomplishing our mission of gender and racial justice in churches. Sheila and I led the community in raising funds to pay travel expenses of participants in order to ensure a diverse group. Clergy, denominational, and seminary leaders across the country from various races, genders, and ten denominations participated in this conference. We worshiped together, addressed the interlocking injustices of sexism and racism, formed small groups to develop specific strategies for change, and celebrated our varied stories. It was the most integrated, inclusive faith community gathering I have ever experienced.

Equity for Women in the Church Community has become incorporated with a board of directors representing various races, genders, and denominations. When we face challenges from differences in theology within the community, we engage in conversations guided by mutual respect and understanding of our varied cultural contexts.

Through Equity for Women in the Church I have my fullest experience of an intercultural faith community. Because we have been intentional about bringing people of various cultures together for mutual interaction and learning from one another, we experience the transforming power of intercultural community.

Experiences and Reflections of Contributors

Intercultural Ministry: Hope for a Changing World includes stories, reflections, and theologies of pastors, theologians, and teachers of varied races, genders, denominations, ages, and ministries. They describe the challenges and rewards of their intercultural ministries. They explore theological foundations for intercultural churches and ministry, provide strategies for building them, and express their hopes for intercultural churches and ministry to advance racial equality, justice, and reconciliation.

This book explores different forms of intercultural ministry so that we can find inspiration and new ways to build intercultural churches and engage in intercultural ministries. It challenges older models of ministry which are monocultural or ethnocentric. In addition, this book explores creative strategies and opportunities for intercultural ministry. Although resistance may be strong, the possibilities for intercultural ministry are stronger as we join together in the Holy Spirit's work of transformation. *Intercultural Ministry* urges us to claim our prophetic calling to make reality the gospel vision of radically inclusive love and justice, a vision of hope for a changing world.

Notes

1. Mark Chaves and Shawna L. Anderson, "Changing American Congregations: Findings from the Third Wave of the National Congregations Study" (October 2014), manuscript draft, accessed October 19, 2016, http://www.soc.duke.edu/natcong/Docs/Changing_American_Congs.pdf; published in *Journal for the Scientific Study of Religion* 53: 676–86.

2. Reginald Bibby, *The Bibby Report: Social Trends Canadian Style* (Toronto: Stoddart Publishing, 1995), 35, 36.

3. Vitor Westhelle, "Multiculturalism, Postcolonialism, and the Apocalyptic," in *Theology and the Religions: A Dialogue*, ed. Viggo Mortensen (Grand Rapids, MI: Eerdmans, 2003), 8.

4. Karen Piper, "Post-Colonialism in the United States: Diversity or Hybridity?," in *Post-Colonial Literatures: Expanding the Canon*, ed. Deborah L. Madsen, Post-Colonial Studies (London: Pluto Press, 1999), 16, 17.

5. "Defining Multicultural, Cross-cultural, and Intercultural," The United Church of Canada/L'Eglise Unie du Canada. Licenses under Creative Commons Attribution Non-commercial No Derivatives (by-nc-nd) Licence. 2011, p. 2.

6. Ibid.

7. Monica A. Coleman, "Knowing a Savior by What She Does," in *She Lives! Sophia Wisdom Works in the World*, Jann Aldredge-Clanton (Woodstock, VT: SkyLight Paths Publishing, 2014), 166.

8. Jann Aldredge-Clanton, *In Search of the Christ-Sophia: An Inclusive Christology for Liberating Christians* (Austin, TX: Eakin Press, 2004), 111.

PART 1

Building Theological Foundations for Intercultural Churches and Ministries

CHAPTER 1

Becoming the Beloved Community

Rev. Dr. Amy Butler

In my first year as senior minister of The Riverside Church in New York City, I attended the funeral of a lifelong member who had met every senior minister in the church's eighty-five-year history, including Harry Emerson Fosdick. Her son, who also grew up in the church, gave the eulogy and recounted hearing Dr. King preach his oft-quoted admonition that 11 o'clock Sunday morning is the most segregated hour of the week. The son said he and his friends would hear this and look around at each other—children of all races, ethnicities, and backgrounds—in utter confusion. The church they knew was wonderfully diverse and in no way reflected the reality Dr. King described.

For some churches, questions around diversity and interculturalism face them every Sunday morning as the pastor looks out on faces that all resemble each other. For other churches, the questions are no less urgent but may be more subtle. Yes, we are comfortable with people who look different from us, but what about people who worship differently—who dislike traditional hymns or love a time of corporate confession? What about people who hold a different theology of atonement or political ideology? When we say all are welcome, do we really mean *all*?

This is a crisis facing the American church and one we have no choice but to address. At a practical level, the demographics of the country are shifting. As we quickly approach a time when whites are no longer the racial majority, churches that do not figure out how to be diverse worshiping bodies are segregating themselves into irrelevance and diminishing congregation size. At a theological level, the church is called to strive to be a reflection of the kindom family of God on earth as in heaven. Our entire purpose of existence is to reflect the heavenly banquet where all are welcomed and know they are loved. We cannot do this without living out the gospel's radical mandate of love in our pews Sunday morning, in our public witness, and in our individual daily lives.

But what do diversity and interculturalism look like? Honestly, they look uncomfortable. They look like cultivating a high tolerance for unease. Living in community is not easy. There is a reason we seek out people who are like us—we are comfortable with what we know. But living in community with a diversity of people, each made in the image of God, is how we more fully catch glimpses of a God we can never fully know.

Institutional Integrity and Interculturalism

On November 24, 2014, a grand jury in Ferguson, Missouri, decided there would be no trial for Officer Darren Wilson, who shot and killed eighteen-year-old Michael Brown. Everything began to change for me in that moment, because the day-to-day work of the pastorate became increasingly overshadowed by those questions of institutional integrity and relevance that we're all asking and have been asking for some time. Is there a future for the church?

It's nice to preach a sermon on Sunday, make a few hospital visits, and show up for the young adult potluck. But those questions come—and you know them: *What is the role of the church in the most pressing crises of our society? What relevance, if any, does the church have for a society that is fractured and segregated? To what extent can the church help bridge the gap between us that breeds fear and hatred?* Those questions wouldn't stay in the background anymore. They kept elbowing their way to the front of the conversation with increasing stridence. And as I saw the tears and pain, grief and hopelessness of my congregation and community in response to events on the news, I kept being reminded: these are not theoretical questions.

Shortly after that verdict was returned, with all of these questions and more filling waking hours and sleepless nights, I boarded a plane with some faith leaders from around the country and spent twenty-four hours in St. Louis, Missouri. During that trip, we were immersed in learning about deeply flawed government, judicial, educational, financial, law enforcement, and other systems in that community. We went to the courthouse in downtown St. Louis, where in 1852, Dred Scott, his wife, Harriet, and their two daughters, Eliza and Lizzie, were denied their freedom and very personhood.

From there we saw unaccredited schools in poor, minority neighborhoods, vast buildings of the prison industrial complex in America, sacred Native American burial mounds flattened—to build a highway. We drove to the site where Michael Brown died, where his body lay in the street for four and a half hours, where there were piles of stuffed animals and cards and makeshift crosses over the blood stains on the road. Finally, we gathered in a church basement, where we listened to young organizers talk about what they were doing and why. Their voices were steady, their commitment clear. And while they knew they were talking with faith leaders, you could tell that didn't impress them one bit. In fact, the more they talked the more their message became obvious: the church is not showing up. The church has no relevance for me, for my life, for this moment, for the injustice and brokenness and despair that colors my very existence. None. All our potlucks and hospital visits and meticulously planned worship services are doing nothing to stop Michael Brown from dying in the middle of the street.

On the way back to the hotel we rode down Florissant Street in Ferguson, where most of the buildings are boarded up and dark, and then past the beautiful new police station. Outside the station, a row of national guardsmen in full riot gear lined up shoulder to shoulder holding automatic weapons and blocking the entrance. Across a parking lot stood a small crowd of peaceful protestors who had determined not to stop showing up since August 9, 2014, when Michael Brown was killed.

It couldn't have been more than twenty feet that separated the two groups, but it was clear that the space between them was filled by more than asphalt and concrete. It was filled with dark, anxious nights of tear gas and smashed-in storefronts. It was filled with generations of misunderstanding and mistrust, filled with injustice born of ignorance, fear, hatred, and apathy, filled with the legacy of broken systems and broken families, filled with the memories of sons and fathers, mothers and daughters of both law enforcement and civilians alike who would never return home again. That narrow gap of street held the original sin of our nation, and the sin of our fallen humanity, even the sin of the church.

Everyone sat in the darkness of the bus, silent for the rest of the ride. As I struggled to process the experience, I wondered if those colleagues riding with me were thinking the same thing I was: we know the church, the institution we've been handed, its grand history and legacy. In this new day, is there anything of any substance and transformative power that the church can offer the world as it is?

I returned home with these questions burning inside me, only to discover that they were waiting for me when I stepped off the plane. The day I returned from Ferguson, another grand jury, this time in my own backyard of Staten Island, returned no indictment for the officer who choked Eric Garner to death.

The Power of Invitation

In a world that considers cathedrals of stone and even the pulpit where Dr. King spoke irrelevant, what is the future of the church? In the fourth chapter of the Gospel of Luke, Jesus comes out of forty days of temptation in the wilderness and, for all his doubts and fears about what was ahead of him, he was determined to begin, filled with the Holy Spirit, a celebrity all over the Galilean countryside.

I think that Jesus, having grown up going to synagogue with his parents from the time he was a young child, had a high regard for the institution and the history, legacy, and message it represented, because when he got ready to kick things off, to start his ministry in earnest, that's where he went. Jesus marched right into that storied institution and stood up to read ancient words that had, perhaps, become a little rote. They were the words of Isaiah, words about bringing good news to the poor, releasing the captives, letting the oppressed go free, words written by a prophet who believed that people of faith were just the ones to do that critical work. And when Jesus finished reading, the text says that "the eyes of all in the synagogue were fixed on him" (Luke 4:20, NRSV). Maybe they all sat in silence, watching with skepticism because, like us, nobody there believed those things could ever happen with any integrity or power.

But Jesus wasn't buying that. "Today this scripture has been fulfilled in your hearing," he declared, which seems to me to say: all the promise, possibility, and power of God's invitation to reconciliation with one another is right here—you just heard it. Whatever it looks like to restore sight to the blind, to proclaim the year of God's favor—this is still our work.

Fast forward two thousand years or so, and here we are again, hearing the ancient words of our holy text with dubious ears. Never mind young, secular organizers and protestors in Ferguson; even *we* don't often buy the possibility of faith communities holding power for transformation—or even, most days, any relevance. But the church can do this. We must. We must work to create communities in which we consistently do the hard work of justice and reconciliation, where we model for the world the possibility of beloved community. If you think for just a few minutes about your best experiences of church, you will know that we can; we can step up into a future we cannot see and be people who make the kind of healing and reconciliation Jesus invited real, and true.

The Gift of Relationship

A few years ago in my church in Washington, DC, we were facing some serious issues of conflict, broken relationship, and an inability to understand one another around the issue of immigration. We were together trying to cultivate diverse community in a city with the largest concentration of undocumented immigrants from El Salvador, together with federal employees who were tasked with the enforcement of severe immigration laws, including routine detention and deportation.

In our church, many of these people sat in worship together at 11 o'clock every Sunday, but as issues around immigration enforcement and reform began to escalate nationally, it was clear that tensions outside our walls were increasingly making their way into the life of our faith community. What could we do? There were relationships on the verge of fracturing, programs we'd worked for together poised to fail, the health of our community on the line.

And so, with some prayer and thought, wise leaders in our community began organizing conversations. There were little house meetings all over the city, where eight to ten people from diverse backgrounds would agree to hear one another's stories over a meal on an evening together. Just one evening, just a small group of people.

The house meeting I attended was an experience I will never forget. About a dozen people were there: a few single folks, one gay man who came with his partner and who worked at a very high level at Immigration and Customs Enforcement (ICE), a family of four undocumented immigrants from El Salvador, and my kids and me. I didn't know what to think when I walked in that night, but as the evening unfolded I swear I saw something that, for me, embodied just what Jesus was talking about when he read those ancient words of promise and insisted they were coming to be right then and there.

The mother in the family from El Salvador began to talk about her life there, why she and her husband—both college-educated teachers—decided to risk everything to bring their two children, then three and eleven, across the border to the United States, where they might have a shot at avoiding the violence and gang culture in which they were immersed in their rural village, where they all might have a chance at a different future.

She talked haltingly and with tears, while her now nineteen-year-old elder son translated, about saving and saving and scraping together the money it would take to hire a *coyote* (a guide) to get them across the Colorado River into Texas, where they would try to make it to their families. They traveled through treacherous terrain, threats of the violence they were trying to leave behind dogging them at every step; pushing their young children to walk endlessly in the heat; running out of water and food; being taken advantage of at every opportunity, until finally they arrived at the river and got ready to cross.

She spoke then about the fear—dread, really—of navigating the rushing current. They were holding onto a rope, she said, one by one, following the guide through the river. Her husband was up ahead of her, leading their eleven-year-old. She was toward the rear, with the three-year-old strapped to her back. Suddenly, about halfway across, he slipped off. Her baby slipped off and the current caught him and pulled him away, out of her grasp, under the rushing water.

By this time in her story, the entire room was silent. Her son, who was translating, could only speak in a halting whisper, too choked up with the memory. Her husband sat in silence, his head in his hands.

She continued: she let go of the rope and went after her baby, of course. Diving under the water she managed to grab a pant leg and desperately, with all her strength, pull him back to her. Together they came up gasping, the baby crying, the current pulling them away from the rest of the family.

In the end, they made it across. And they made it through many other harrowing experiences to the safety of family in the DC area, where they began to build a life from scratch. Both parents work as hourly laborers, their children now nineteen and eleven.

It was a stunning story, but the most stunning thing of all is that this was no anonymous recounting. We were all in tears with the power of their story and realized that right there, on the couch across the room from us, sat people with whom we worshiped every Sunday. And to think that eleven-year-old David, who brightens up the Sunday school every single week, loves to sing in the children's choir, and hugs me at the door after worship on Sundays, could have been lost—these are people we *love*!

I think we all got to a common ground that night, though we were by all appearances so very different from one another. We managed to move across the divide of misunderstanding and pain to suddenly realize that the gift of those relationships is so deeply worth the pain of learning to understand each other.

This is the hard work of the beloved community. When we do that hard, hard work of living in relationship, in community, in *church* with people we love, we find we *can* stand in the divide of policy, opinion, and political persuasion, and somehow, some way, we can bridge a gap that seemed totally unbridgeable before.

This is beloved community. This is the kin-dom of God. This is what the world needs. This is the church.

The Courage to Change

Many people wonder about the future of the church. *I* wonder about the future of the church. But in all of that wondering, what has become clear to me, both on a theoretical level and on a deeply intimate level, is that the world, that all of us, desperately need the best expression of the church.

But maybe what we don't need is an institution as we have come to know it. Maybe what we need is for the church to take up the core of its identity, return to why it came to be in the first place and what we so deeply believe about our role in God's redemptive work in the world, and have a hand-off: let go of the trappings of the past in whatever way we must in order to become, again, the beloved community.

What does that look like? Standing on the side of the oppressed? Yes, of course; this is our ancient, foundational, and urgent call. But I think the church this world most desperately needs is going to have to do more than that. If we want to bring what we believe to real and transformative life, we need more. The people sitting in the pews need more. The police need more. Those young organizers in Ferguson need more. Everyone who hasn't thought of going to church in years needs more.

It is easy for us to hear the stories I've told and feel compelled to join a march to advocate for racial justice or the undocumented; many of us have done just that very recently. But it's harder to stand with protesters and reach out to the police department. It is harder for the undocumented mother and the ICE official to serve Communion together. It is harder for us to look around the church and think about inviting into covenant not just those we don't know, but those we see every week but would prefer not to. As followers of Jesus Christ, however, we must stand in the gap, bridge the divide, because if the first time we are meeting those who are different from us is in the street in protest and anger after another tragedy, then we have failed.

The call of the church is deeper and harder than what we have become in society. The call of the church is to stand in the gap, modeling and facilitating hard and painful conversations, midwifing the birth of common ground when the divides are so deep and the pain so raw and the perspectives so different that there seems to be no hope.

And my faith in the church starts to come into focus when I think of the times when divides, when gaps, when other kinds of separations begin to show within the Christian community. Believe me, this moment in history is not the first time the church has had a division or a separation. If there is an institution on the planet that understands division, healing from division, and coming together once more as a community, it is the church of Jesus Christ.

We see in the biblical witness that the church has moved to do the hard work of reconciliation, to model beloved community for the world. We can see it in the stories of even the first church, when, after Jesus left, there arose serious dissension.

A schism divided two camps, and each felt deeply convicted that their position was the right position. One camp was led by the apostle Paul, who was of the opinion that the gospel message was one that should be proclaimed to the whole world—not just in Jerusalem and the surrounding regions where Jesus preached and lived—and that everyone should be welcomed in. Leading the other camp was the apostle Simon Peter. Peter was convinced that if you decided you believed in Jesus, the first step you would take was, of course, to convert to Judaism. You'd go through all the rites of Jewish identity and assume an upright Jewish lifestyle with all the dietary restrictions and Levitical rules that entailed.

And this controversy was the backdrop for the amazing story Luke reports in the tenth chapter of Acts, the story of Peter and Cornelius.

Cornelius was a centurion of the Italian Cohort, which meant that Cornelius was an extremely high-ranking official in the Roman army, not only a Gentile but also a leader of the occupying forces in Jerusalem and surrounding areas. Cornelius was not a Jew and had no interest in becoming a Jew. In fact, converting to Judaism would have been grounds for immediate dismissal from the Roman army. But he is described in the book of Acts as "a devout man who feared God" (Acts 10:2, NRSV). And one day, as Cornelius was praying, he heard God's voice telling him to search out a man called Simon Peter . . . and so he did.

Meanwhile, Simon Peter was staying at the house of a friend on the seashore in Joppa, and he went up on the roof, as was his custom, for his daily prayer time. He also had a vision, but this one was a little stranger than Cornelius's vision. Peter, devout Jew and committed follower of Jesus Christ, saw a sheet coming down from heaven. On the sheet were all kinds of animals, even animals clearly named in the Levitical code, the Jewish law, as unclean. The voice Peter heard was a voice telling him to kill . . . and eat the animals provided to him for food.

Well, you can imagine how shocking this was. No way was Peter going to breach Jewish law to do something he had learned his entire life was unclean and forbidden. Peter knew that there were certain standards for faithful, holy living. And he could recite them front to back.

But then Peter heard the voice again, and this time he knew it was God. God had stern words for poor Peter, and they were: "What God has called clean . . . you *must not* call profane" (Acts 10:15, NRSV, emphasis added).

In that moment there was a knock on Peter's door, and the men sent by Cornelius asked him to come to Caesarea at Cornelius's request. Peter was so shaken and so compelled by the vision he'd seen that he went to Cornelius's house. Upon arriving, Peter began to preach to a large, assembled crowd: "You yourselves know that it is unlawful for a Jew to associate with or to visit a Gentile; but God has shown me that I should not call anyone profane or unclean" (Acts 10:28, NRSV).

This was shocking—a complete 180 for Simon Peter. He had dug his heels in to maintain his position of conviction, but miraculously, he had now revised his opinion.

As Peter explained his conversion to the gathered crowd, the text says that the Holy Spirit fell on the crowd. Now, I am not sure what that looked like—maybe something like what happened on Pentecost with the crowd speaking different languages. But it's the end result that's so deeply amazing.

The community changed course.

The whole group.

The church shifted; the institution revised its direction in response to the leadership of God's Spirit. They looked at each other and said: "Can anyone withhold the water for baptizing these people who have received the Holy Spirit just as we have?" (Acts 10:47, NRSV).

God's Spirit blew right in and the people listened. And their courageous corporate response to what was a fundamental shift swung wide the doors of the church to welcome everyone, and it changed the entire future of the church of Jesus Christ.

This characteristic, this ability to shift direction with agility, is not, shall we say, a particularly common quality in institutions like the church. In fact, one might say that institutions are fundamentally incompatible with this quality of course correction. Institutions thrive on static bureaucracy. We like policies. And bylaws. And procedures and constitutions and handbooks and rules.

And we need all of these things. But the church must shift in the area of radical welcome to become an institution that leads the world in the work of reconciliation. I desperately hope that this is the church we are becoming, coming together across racial, theological, and cultural divides to form covenants of action that have the potential to transform our communities. Because this is the unique call of the church. We know how to do this, because we follow the One who modeled sacrifice and love at all costs, who called us, not to institutional preservation or strategic congregational growth, but to hard, tear-filled, trusting, healing relationship—to becoming the beloved community.

The deep and foundational tragedy of Ferguson and Staten Island and so many other places across our country is that people who live and work and raise families in the same neighborhoods do not know each other, do not understand each other, and therefore cannot love each other.

The world doesn't know how to do this, but we know how to do this, Church. Nobody knows it better. We have to have those hard conversations at all costs. We must find a way to bridge these divides. We have to become, again and again, the beloved community. It's in our DNA; it's in our Holy Scripture; it's in the best expressions of our history and tradition; it's in the very call of almighty God to so many who have gone before us.

A colleague of mine tells the story of an inner-city priest who, after years of seeing the local gang claim too many children to lives of violence and crime, confronted the gang leader and told him he was not going to stand by any longer. The gang leader's response was sobering. He said, "You will lose, and I will win. Because when these children walk to school in the morning, I am there, and when they come home in the afternoon, I am there. When they play in the playgrounds and run errands for their parents, I am there. I am there and you are not and I win."

Whether our communities are plagued by gang violence or poverty, predatory lending or deportation threats, too many of our neighbors look at the hopelessness of the world around them and believe the words of Jesus can't possibly be true. They believe there is no release for the captives, no sight for the blind. They believe this because we haven't been there to show them any differently.

This is our gospel mandate. We must come out of our pulpits and into the streets, into the gaps of broken relationship and broken trust. But first, we must create communities that live intentionally in the dis-ease of difference and welcome the radical reconciliation of God's Spirit.

CHAPTER 2

The Church's Prophetic Call to Steward Our Collective Memory

Rev. Brandon Green

For me as a black pastor, the notion of intercultural churches causes a warring set of convictions to bubble up within me. On one hand I believe intercultural communities of faith are the fruit of the gospel. Theologically it's hard to make a case otherwise. We read in Acts 2 what it looks like when the Spirit of God descends on humanity and establishes a community of believers. In Acts we get a vision of a beautiful community of diversity, reciprocity, and interdependence. We get to see folks hearing the gospel in their own tongues; we get to see the church as it could be—or better yet, as it should be.

It is this ideal and this hope that has shaped my sense of calling and commitment to ministry. I serve as associate pastor of River City Community Church, where I have been in leadership in some capacity for more than a decade. River City is an intercultural church located in west Humboldt Park, a neighborhood on the west side of Chicago, one of America's most segregated cities. It is to this ministry that I intend to give my life; however, I do so fully aware of a very real tension—a bifurcation that is within me.

That is where the conflict mentioned above finds its root. I have come to be suspicious of anything labeled "intercultural" or "diverse" or "reconciliation," as they have often become buzz-words that represent nothing more than a superficially diverse gathering of people. Cynically I observe these gatherings, and walk away with the opinion that they are diverse only in regards to the individual cultures people abandoned in order to belong to these "intercultural" communities.

This mindset is not exclusive to me. I'm reminded of a time I was preparing a sermon; I decided to bounce some of my ideas off the brothers I play basketball with. They asked me, "What are you preaching on?" I responded quickly and proudly: "Reconciliation." I sat there in anticipation of their thoughts. A few seconds went by, and then they started to giggle. As they were laughing, I became irritated and asked abruptly, "What are you laughing at?" They responded, "You go to a white church, don't you?" I asked, "Why would you say that?"

The assumption the brothers held was that I must attend a white church or in some way be invested in whiteness in order to care about reconciliation, because in their minds "reconciliation isn't for us; it's the concern of white folks." Now some of these brothers were Christian men, so it was common for me to discuss church with them. In fact, it was so common that they gave me the nickname "Preach." So their hesitancy to broach this subject matter was not because of their distrust of things Christian but of things deemed white. The question they raised was: How can we begin to talk about a common future if we have not owned up to the past? They warned that pursuing reconciliation in this way, without a common understanding of the past, is to do so on white folk's terms.

Jennifer Harvey, in *Dear White Christians*, says: "White Christians' concerns about our segregated [church] hour overwhelmingly rest on the unspoken assumption that inclusion of diversification should happen primarily in one direction. Namely, 'our' churches are too white and the fact that they do not include more people of color probably means racism is present." Harvey goes on to say that "the reconciliation paradigm often succumbs and becomes overly attentive to white concerns at the expense of the concerns and needs of communities of color."[1]

Harvey communicates what the brothers at the gym knew intuitively. Reconciliation without a clear understanding of the needed reciprocity destines those in the pursuit of reconciliation to do so on preexisting constructs of power, ultimately rendering this endeavor toward reconciliation to be nothing more than a nuanced and complicated captivity for people of color.

I walked away from those brothers conceding that there is some truth to their assertion. When I began this work in ministry, I sought out black pastors who were leading intercultural communities of faith, and I have found very few. I began to wonder if maybe the guys at the gym understand this bifurcated reality better than I do. They seemed uninterested in living with the tension intercultural communities often require of black leaders. Their thoughts caused insecurities to bubble up in me. I started to ask myself, "Has my connection to River City Community Church reduced my capacity to have affinity with my black brothers and sisters? Have I drunk the Kool-Aid? Have I acquiesced my identity in hopes of finding my place in white spaces?"

James 1:8 asserts that a double-minded person is unstable in all things. I rest firmly in the tensions of what I view as a theological imperative and my very real social location. W. E. B. Du Bois captures my sentiment when addressing the inherent tension intercultural communities present for me:

> It is a peculiar sensation, this double consciousness, this sense of always looking at one's self through the eyes of others, of measuring one's soul by the tape of a world that looks on in amused contempt and pity. One ever feels [one's] two-ness,— an American, a Negro; two souls, two thoughts, two unreconciled strivings; two warring ideals in one dark body, whose dogged strength alone keeps it from being torn asunder.[2]

Du Bois articulates the two-ness or double-ness of being an American and being black. This draws out the truth that in some way my blackness excludes me from things American. The term "African American" is often deemed a hyphenation; Du Bois articulates it as bifurcation. I think that same two-ness exists within the pews and is propagated from the pulpit and made manifest throughout the ethos of the church.

I am a Christian beholden to the ideals and the life of Christ, yet I am a black Christian. In church circles I must sadly confess that my experiences are not of inclusion or hyphenation but of bifurcation. There are truly two souls, two thoughts, two unreconciled strivings, with two different iterations of the past, bringing out these warring ideals in me. This environment that produces this two-ness in me and others in the church is one of the manifestations of the church's captivity.

Soong-Chan Rah defines what I mean by captivity: "the phrase 'captivity of the church' points to the danger of the church being defined by an influence other than scriptures."[3] For most of our history, the evangelical church in the United States has reflected and internalized the values of white American culture. As a person of color, what am I to do? If my seminaries are white, my church is white with a white theology that communicates indirectly that my messiah is white. While never said explicitly (anymore), it is implied that my culture and ethnicity and their inherent values are sin, and that to be saved I must become white. As a person of color, to exist in an intercultural church setting is to do so with this two-ness. People of color who willingly enter into intercultural communities of faith are charged with the responsibility/ burden of navigating the micro, sometimes macro, aggressions of this world and the micro/macro aggressions of a gospel influenced by dominant culture.

I am indeed a double-minded man as it relates to intercultural communities of faith. The tension of this two-ness as captured by Du Bois is very real to me, yet so is the call of the gospel. I long deeply to see the prayer of Jesus in John 17:21 be answered: that we would be one. I believe this two-ness, this contradicted self, may be the reason the brothers at the gym had no interest in the notion of racial reconciliation. When we remain in our enclaves of homogeneity, we can protect ourselves better from this level of severing that occurs. In homogenous settings we don't wrestle with a hyphenated self. We aren't bifurcated—we just are.

One of the guiding questions for this chapter was "What is the future and hope of intercultural ministry?" This question is challenging, but I wonder if one of the favorite shows of my children helps to begin to answer the question. In the movie *The Prince of Egypt* there is a song called "When You Believe." One of the lines says, "Though hope is frail, it's hard to kill." This is part of my answer to the question on the future of intercultural ministries. Though my hope is frail, it is still living.

It is my belief that intercultural communities are God's clearly expressed ideal. The church's inability to build intercultural community lies in our reluctance to claim our prophetic responsibility and define a reality rooted in a common past. In December 2007, during an oversight hearing of the Congressional Committee on the Judiciary, Bishop M. Thomas Shaw of the Episcopal Church spoke these words: "With fuller knowledge [of our history] will come true repentance that will then open us to reconciliation and remedies that we believe are yet to be revealed."[4]

We as the collective church don't share a common vision toward wholeness. We fail to see a common future, because we lack a common past. Georges Erasmus, aboriginal leader from Canada, said, "Where common memory is lacking, where people do not share in the same past, there can be no real community. Where community is to be formed, common memory must be created."[5] When we refuse to remember together, we do the opposite—we dismember. Integral in the formation of intercultural communities is the need for a common memory that informs our present reality.

Defining Reality

How do we define reality together? I've been blessed to be part of a community that has taken great strides in making our church a house of prayer for all nations. In our efforts to do this, we often have conversations or lectures on the state of race in our country, city, neighborhood, and congregation. Power, privilege, reconciliation, slavery, and economics inevitably come up. Our community is well versed in intercultural dialogue and its rhetoric, at least to the point where everyone kind of knows the right thing to say, even if they have a hard time fleshing it out. However, once in awhile when we engage the topic of slavery, we get a few voices asking us to move on from the past and live in the present. To which I always ask, "Whose definition of the 'present' do we live in? Whose history informs this 'present' reality?"

It is interesting that, during every election cycle, all we hear from candidates is how the past informs their policy or campaign ideals. Yet when we have these conversations on how we are going to lead our congregation and our communities into an intercultural future, we want to disallow the past or seek to control its narrative. It then becomes a competition as to who gets to define our past or through whose lens we get to gaze upon our history, holding in the balance the power to shape our present.

I trace this line of thinking back to the garden of Eden. In the beginning God created the heavens and the earth, and all of creation was good and was deemed good because creation reflected the character and image of God.

The temptation in the garden wasn't just about knowledge. The temptation at its core was to be like God, to be able to create and define reality based on who we are. Adam and Eve ate the fruit, and immediately we can see the consequences. They started to redefine their reality. Being vulnerable or naked became wrong. Their decision caused a change in their relationship with God as well; the sound of God in the garden induced fear rather than joy. It also changed their relationship with creation; instead of stewarding creation, responsibility turned to blame. They discounted their entire history with God's provision and reciprocal love.

Their world was changed, as was their worldview. I think what is lost in the narrative about Adam and Eve is the ecological effect of their sin. When Adam and Eve partook of the forbidden fruit, they unleashed a dysfunction that had cataclysmic consequences on all of creation. The entire system of the world changed in that moment. Creation was no longer reciprocal or interdependent. The relationship between humanity and creation was relegated to a utilitarian coexistence, and their relationship with God became one filled with fear and distrust. There was a shift in the ecosystem. Things that once experienced perpetual existence, continuity, and community now are isolated and finite. Sin entered their world and changed everything. I believe this narrative has more of an impact on us than we give credence, and it has influenced our current conditions.

Racism is but the outworking of humanity's desire to define our reality. Race is a social construct, an apparatus to carry out racist ideals. Professor Ian F. Haney Lopez puts it this way:

> I define a "race" as a vast group of people loosely bound together by historically contingent, socially significant elements of their morphology and/or ancestry. . . . Race is neither an essence nor an illusion, but rather an ongoing, contradictory, self-reinforcing process subject to the macro forces of social and political struggle and the micro effects of daily decisions.[6]

The original sin of racism led to the categorization of people for the purpose of delineating their humanity. The construct of race is an attempt to redefine our reality without the influence of God's image and character. Race, however, has evolved into something more than a social construct. It's a living organism; it's more like Frankenstein's monster. By that, I mean racism is engrained in the fabric and system of American society. The individual racist need not exist to note that institutional racism is pervasive in the dominant culture.[7] Race is a human-made invention, but humanity has lost control of it. It's a monster that continues to wreak havoc, one we cannot seem to stop. This mutation evolves, and its presence changes the world it resides in.

If indeed the development of the social construct of race is America's original sin, then the cataclysmic event that has changed our world is the invention of white supremacy.

According to the Oxford dictionary, white supremacy is "the belief that white people are superior to those of all other races, especially the black race, and should therefore dominate society."[8] I think this definition is good, and I would even add: Not only is it a *belief*; it is now part of the very air we breathe. White supremacy is more than individual or systemic; it's atmospheric. And if that is true, then we cannot forget its ecological effects, either historically or in its current manifestations. It infects and permeates all other subsequent social constructs; it taints our judicial, educational, and economic systems, creating and shaping our values and ethics. Its reach is comprehensive. It has demented our theology so as to harmonize with our broken society. It is pervasive and relentless; it infects all cultures it is in contact with.

Recently I listened to two black men debating about how "black" somebody was. It struck me in that moment that when we participate in the delineation or evaluation of one another's blackness, it is an act of affirming a race paradigm initiated by white supremacy. By simply entertaining this "blacker-than-thou" mentality and engaging in the conversation itself, we are validating this constructed reality. When this is brought to our attention, it is tempting to defend our actions as if our comments have inherent objective truth to them. Ironically, the reason for such an exercise is to somehow escape white supremacy; yet it is when we gradate the humanity of our brothers and sisters and their proximity to blackness, we find ourselves emitting toxins that sustain the atmosphere of white supremacy. This is true of any other cultural group who would find themselves measuring one another's affinity. We are all subject to the atmosphere of white supremacy.

If we long to construct an environment where intercultural communities can be formed, then we must first admit and accept that we are all infected with white supremacy. Acknowledging this reality is akin to acknowledging that all have sinned and fallen short of the glory of God. With sin, you have to come to God and say, "I am a sinner, and I need to be saved." To be converted into a reconciler, you have to come to God and say, "I have been infected by white supremacy, and I need to be saved." This truth is like the spot on the map that says, "You are here." We cannot begin to etch out our destination if we are oblivious to our current location, and we cannot truly know where we are if we don't have a common memory.

A Common Captivity

Realizing the atmospheric reality of white supremacy gives perspective to the weight of being marginalized in this environment. Living life knowing that every law, every policy ever created in this country has in its DNA an implicit bias toward white superiority is astounding. Knowing that the laws that are meant to ensure our safety and well-being are being produced in an ecosystem designed to rob folks of their humanity by threat of incarceration or death is overwhelming. What's more is that the judicial process I am to submit to in order to advocate against that bias is subject to the same infection of white supremacy. There is no refuge. With that said, what can be done?

I resign myself to believe that the liberation of one person should not be at the expense of another's liberty. Therefore, we can't replace white supremacy with the supremacy of some other group—that only perpetuates the dehumanization of all people. The white supremacy narrative attacks humanity, and its aim is the destruction of the *imago dei*, both for the privileged and the oppressed; likewise, any other construct of supremacy will produce the same end by different means. Whites are held just as much in captivity to the history and narrative of white supremacy as the marginalized.

The problem for us all is that we have not come to recognize the chains. We, the marginalized, have come to idolize the chains of our white brothers and sisters seeking to attain their brand of freedom. I like the way hip-hop artist Talib Kweli phrases it: "We're like slaves on a ship talking about who got the flyest chain."⁹ In this line Kweli captures the inability of those held captive to recognize the complications of their captivity.

Accepting this common memory that validates the history of white supremacy and its atmospheric properties is the initial task. This truth should inform us of the conditions of our confinement. While there is no question that social and economic chains of captivity are far greater for the Native community, the black community, and other communities that have been exploited and disenfranchised, we must still remember that we are all held in captivity. It is not a stretch to say that when you flip the paradigm, the chains that white people are tethered to are even more severely entangled. The lies that call into question the humanity of the marginalized are the same chains that bind our white brothers' and sisters' identity to this system. As I stated earlier, race is comparable to Frankenstein's monster; it cares nothing about its creators or their offspring. Its only aim is to crush, diminish, and distort the *imago dei* in all of us.

The chains of white supremacy and the various cultures it forms have been significant contributors in defining reality. Our chains have become our birthright; we sometimes find that our chains feel too good. Our captivity has been normalized and has been deemed right. Chains in this captivity are heirlooms passed on from the previous generations. To detach ourselves from these chains is to detach ourselves from a culture of sin that has been established and romanticized for generations. As the dominant culture clings to their chains of power and privilege and the marginalized to their chains of victimhood and the entitlement and exemptions associated with being a victim, we submerge ourselves into a deeper captivity.

The conditions of our imprisonment have significant ramification. In the words of Dr. King, "Our individual freedom is inextricably bound to the freedom of every soul on earth."[10] This is a sobering reality. King communicates that liberation for all people is predicated on reconciliation. We can never experience true freedom if our white brothers and sisters cling to their chains, and the marginalized to ours.

James H. Cone put it this way in *God of the Oppressed*:

> To be liberated is to be delivered from the state of unfreedom to freedom; it is to have the chains struck off the body and mind so that the creature of God can be who he or she is. Reconciliation is that bestowal of freedom and life with God which takes place on the basis of God's liberating deeds. Liberation and reconciliation are tied together and have meaning only through God's initiative.[11]

A phrase I find poignant in this quote is the phrase "God's liberating deeds." Philippians 2:1-8 reveals God's liberating deeds in the incarnation, life, death, and resurrection of Jesus. Jesus alone has the capacity to define liberation and captivity, for Jesus alone can truly contrast one from the other objectively and with empathy. Jesus understands intimately the captivity of this world; deeper still is Jesus' knowledge and intimacy with the kin-dom of heaven and its liberated reality. Jesus too was a slave, and now is free.

Jesus is our Harriet Tubman, coming back and inviting us to walk out of our captivity, but we first have to acknowledge we are trapped by something. We can't follow Jesus into the underground railroad of freedom until we realize we are in absolute captivity.

According to Cone, our current atmospheric condition of white supremacy is blasphemous. "God is no longer God unless the creature of God is delivered from that which is enslaving and dehumanizing."[12] The conditions we minister under are conditions of dehumanization; the very air we breathe is polluted with toxins aimed at corroding the *imago dei* of God's beloved. To answer the question posed earlier in this chapter, "What is the future and hope of intercultural ministry?" I believe the future of intercultural ministry is tied to the church's willingness to steward its prophetic responsibility.

This to me is our prophetic responsibility: Ours is the call to a common memory that informs our reality and its atmospheric conditions. Ours is a posture of repentance for our complicity and apathy in the shaping of false narratives that have distorted our history. Ours is the remission of the sin of white supremacy—nailing it to the cross. Ours is adherence to the rebuke of Jesus after curing so many; ours is to go and sin no more.

There will be hesitation and pushback to this call, not unlike the response of the Pharisees when Jesus entered into humanity to call his people to a common memory. All throughout the Gospels we hear Jesus reference the prophets and the law of Moses, asking his people to come to this place of commonness, to remember together. It was their shared history that he sought to build his ministry on. However, Jesus' intention of awakening God's people from their collective amnesia was received with anger and defensiveness. The Pharisees had a great deal to lose if they were to remember together. His call to a common memory would require them to rethink their theology, religious praxis, stewardship of the marginalized, acceptance of the foreigner, gender roles, economics, power, and privilege. If we are to take seriously the call to steward this responsibility, then the church must be honest and courageous about what it stands to lose if we are to embrace this prophetic responsibility. This call should draw out of us lament and repentance, ultimately culminating in reformation. The hope of intercultural churches is predicated on the degree to which the church is capable of calling God's people to a common memory: a memory that informs the way we understand our present and shapes the way we pursue our future.

Notes

1. Jennifer Harvey, *Dear White Christians: For Those Still Longing for Racial Reconciliation* (Grand Rapids, MI: Eerdmans, 2014), Kindle locations 1592–1595.

2. W. E. B. Du Bois, *The Souls of Black Folk* (Chicago: A. C. McClurg & Company, 1903), 9–10.

3. Soong-Chan Rah, *The Next Evangelicalism: Freeing the Church from Western Cultural Captivity* (Downers Grove, IL: IVP Books, 2009), 127.

4. The Right Reverend M. Thomas Shaw III, SSJE, "Oversight Hearing on the Legacy of the Trans-Atlantic Slave Trade," transcript from Committee on the Judiciary, Subcommittee on the Constitution, Civil Rights, and Civil Liberties, December 18, 2007, 3, accessed October 20, 2016, http://www.episcopalchurch.org/library/article/too-many-episcopalians-were-silent-slavery-massachusetts-bishop-tells-congressional.

5. Georges Erasmus, "Essays in Public Theology: Collected Essays 1," *Theology and the Transformation of Culture* 1 (2007), 191.

6. Ian F. Haney Lopez, "The Social Construction of Race: Some Observations on Illusion, Fabrication, and Choice," *29 Harvard Civil Rights-Civil Liberties Law Review* (Winter 1994), 12.

7. "Racism," accessed March 17, 2016, http://www.merriam-webster.com/dictionary/racism.

8. *Oxford Dictionary of English*, accessed October 20, 2016, https://en.oxforddictionaries.com/definition/us/white_supremacy.

9. Talib Kweli, "Reflection Eternal/Africa Dream," MP3 (Electric Lady Studios, 2000).

10. Martin Luther King Jr., "Letter from a Birmingham Jail," January 3, 1964, accessed November 18, 2016, https://web.cn.edu/kwheeler/documents/Letter_Birmingham_Jail.pdf.

11. James H. Cone, *God of the Oppressed*, Kindle ed. (Maryknoll, NY: Orbis Books, 1997), kindle location 4133 of 5323.

12. Cone, *God of the Oppressed*.

CHAPTER 3

Disrupting Babylon

Rev. Emily McGinley

Some people might call me a race traitor.[1]

But, then again, the kind of people who would say that are probably right. As a *hapa haole*[2] and the daughter of an immigrant mother who grew up a refugee in the ghettos of Taiwan, I should be doing everything I can to climb the ladder of privilege and power—if not for my sake, then for hers. And maybe I would have, if it hadn't been for my conversion to Christianity as a teenager.

It happened in a typical evangelical and conservative church in a medium-sized, working-class town in Washington State. They were contentedly unaware of their White[3] supremacy and soft racism,[4] but what I did gain from it was access to a different way of being in the world. The gospel I was introduced to—for better and worse—told me that this world did not matter. What mattered was how far you were willing to go as a faithful follower of Jesus Christ. And, through that hermeneutical lens, I was introduced to a different way of living, doing, and being in the world; a different set of values than the ones I had been taught and shown in my own family.

And so, when I accepted the path and life as a follower of Jesus, what started out as a tentative step in a new direction became a dramatically life-altering event. Here I am, more than twenty years later, pastoring a congregation I planted on the south side of Chicago. Strange things happen when you take the gospel seriously.

One of the Scripture passages that guides my vocational call comes from Jeremiah 29:4-7:

...the God of Israel proclaims to all the exiles I have carried off from Jerusalem to Babylon: Build houses and settle down; cultivate gardens and eat what they produce. Get married and have children; then help your sons find wives and your daughters find husbands in order that they too may have children. Increase in number there so that you don't dwindle away. Promote the welfare of the city where I have sent you into exile. Pray to God for it, because your future depends on its welfare.

What does it mean to "promote the welfare of the city"? On the surface, the instruction might seem obvious: contribute to the economy; engage in civic responsibilities; be an all-around good citizen. But the context of this Scripture is one of a community living in exile, a community that is grieving loss, a community that has been coopted and colonized for the service of a conquering power. It's a community negotiating the tension between the values they hold as a people united by God's promises and being forced to live for an indefinite period among a foreign people with equally foreign values.

Is God calling them to assimilate? At face value, that's what it would seem. But, of course, God does not give up so easily. In fact, God had an even bigger plan in mind. But first, let's talk about ride sharing.

Disrupting Markets

Just a few years ago, if I were planning a trip to the airport, the night before I would pick up the phone and schedule a taxi. These days, of course, I don't call in the night before. Instead, that same morning, about ten to fifteen minutes before I need to leave, I do something else. I pick up my phone and call Uber or Lyft.

Recently, I did just that when I traveled out to San Jose for a wedding. As I stayed at a friend's home, deep in the heart of Silicon Valley, one of the things that we talked about was the trend among start-ups to be disruptors. By disruptors, I mean companies that disrupt existing markets. Disruption can make markets leaner and more effective and can drive innovation. It can also backfire.

Uber is a ride-sharing business and, as such, a disruptor in the transportation industry. Uber is good at disrupting the taxi industry from both ends, from driver to rider. Uber has been wildly successful at infiltrating numerous regional markets, and it has been growing quickly. Except when Uber went to Europe.

In Europe and, ironically, in Germany, Uber—*Über*—failed miserably. Their estimated loss is at $62.5 billion. Why? Europeans thought Uber, as a company, was pushy and offensive—something that a lot of people in the United States also think. The difference was that Europeans were not willing to set that aside in favor of convenience and a good deal. For Germans, in particular, it offended their regard for the common good. If your core value is pure profits, regardless of social impact, Uber wins hands down. But if your core value is the common good—safety laws, licensing and certification laws—Uber becomes problematic.

Conversely, I recently heard about another business, Gravity Payments, a credit card processing and financial services company that became a disruptor in a very different way. Dan Price, cofounder and CEO of Gravity, read a study about how much money people needed to be happy. Influenced by it, he decided to set everyone's salary at the company—120 employees, including his own—to seventy thousand dollars. In doing so, whether he had intended to or not, Gravity Payments became a disruptor of wages.

Price had figured there would be some free publicity, but he did not anticipate the level of backlash that would come with it. A couple of employees left the company because they didn't like the idea of people who were not at the same level as them making the same salary. His brother and cofounder, who owns 30 percent of the company, filed a lawsuit. Other small business owners resented him. Rush Limbaugh—someone that Price grew up listening to regularly in his home-schooled, conservative Christian family—accused him of having a socialist agenda. However, there were plenty of folks excited about this decision. Gravity Payments lost some clients but gained even more. Price received thousands of résumés; talk-show hosts lined up to interview him; Harvard business professors flew out to conduct a case study; and third graders wrote him thank-you notes.

Because of Price's decision, some employees feel free to begin a family; others are able to purchase a home, and one employee can afford to travel and visit her family. Price simply wanted to improve the quality of life for his employees and inject a powerful idea into society: maybe you could run an effective business and still commit to the financial well-being of your community.

Why would you commit to the well-being of others? Maybe it is because you're a good person. Or maybe it is because you are idealistic. Maybe it is because you love your community and want to see it flourish.

So then, back to our earlier question: What does it mean to help your community flourish? What does it mean to "promote the welfare of the city"?

Disrupting Babylon

As I followed my call toward ministry and learned more about the sin of systemic racism and economic injustice, it became ever clearer to me that the welfare of the city depends not so much on increasing the health and strength of Babylon (which is, of course, a placeholder for any ruling power that is built on domination) but rather, disrupting its cycles of capturing, co-opting, and colonizing hearts and minds.

So, what does it look like to disrupt Babylon? It might look like becoming a race traitor. By this, I mean that it might mean choosing to opt out of the incentives and benefits that Babylon extends to individuals in order to maintain systems and structures of power that allow a few to benefit at the cost of many. In the context where I serve as a pastor, this power is often connected to privileges of the majority race but also can include power-laden privileges embedded in sexual orientation, gender identity, educational attainment, and economic status.

I serve as the founding pastor of Urban Village Church (Hyde Park-Woodlawn), the fourth of a multi-site congregation with locations throughout the city of Chicago. Urban Village Church tends to be comprised of millennials, with a concentration of young adults in their twenties and thirties who come from evangelical, mainline, Catholic, charismatic, and even unchurched backgrounds. Our focus on faith in action through service and justice, our expressed inclusivity of those along the spectrum of sexual orientation and gender identity, our stated vision of working toward dismantling racism, and our commitment to helping faith be relevant beyond the church sphere are among the primary reasons why individuals choose to be engaged in our faith community.

In an urban center where realities such as gentrification, underemployment, economic stratification, and declining funding for education, mental health, and physical wellness continue to dehumanize, the need for a vision beyond Babylon grows increasingly urgent with each passing school year, each passing gunshot victim, and each passing election cycle. Reminding people that the power of resurrection through Jesus Christ is greater than the powers of institutional, political, and economic machinery is not just a pleasant sentiment—or even a survival tactic. It is the fuel for disrupting Babylon.

The strategy for disruption comes from Jeremiah 29: Be present. Invest joyfully. Engage critically. Witness faithfully. It all sounds nice enough, but it is a subversive approach to introducing a dramatically different way to do life from what our current structures encourage.

Be Present

One of the norms among young adults in our congregation is transience. Many young people choose to move or find it necessary to move for school, adventure, work, or economic reasons. In a recent study of Wicker Park, a neighborhood in which one of our sites is located, the average stay of a resident was estimated at six months. Many might assume this is just the way things are, without much thought or concern on what impact their transience might have on the neighborhood. In the midst of economic and social forces, it would be easy to be swept along without a second thought.

So then, what does it look like to disrupt Babylon while being carried along? What is the Christian response? *Stay present.* Through the life of Jesus Christ, Christians proclaim a God who chose solidarity over power, community over privilege, relationship over upward mobility. Choosing to commit to a neighborhood, or at least a city, is a tangible embodiment of that kind of solidarity. Choosing to stay rooted in and to build up community is a direct disruption of the forces of gentrification that capitalize on transience and the fragmentation of community.

Invest Joyfully

Choosing to stay, even if only for a few years, requires a joyful investment in the community. Instead of viewing the city solely as an experience and a playground for one's young adult life before moving on, I've encouraged my parishioners to invest in their community—to "plant gardens" by cultivating spaces where life can thrive and to "build houses" by creating places where people can gather and share food and relationship together. Adding to the vibrancy and joy of a community is what creates connections between individuals and helps neighborhoods to flourish.

Another way to think about it is to take the old camping model of leaving a place in better shape than when you arrived. Joyful investment also calls for an understanding of what makes a community so special—including the struggles that have made it what it is. This, in turn, demands critical engagement.

Engage Critically

The power of privilege is that some voices are intentionally given more space, greater amplification, and higher credibility. Disrupting Babylon involves doing the hard work of hearing those voices that get stifled, gaining consciousness, and examining the air we breathe and the waters we swim in. Whether by educating oneself on a neighborhood or city's history of real estate lending and housing distribution or why some areas have greater access to high-quality produce than others, choosing to engage in critical understanding and putting oneself in places where one's worldview is challenged and expanded—things such as taking time to call or visit with local representatives on issues that may or may not be your issues but for which you may be able to lend power and privilege through the amplification of voices that are diminished—this is what critical engagement looks like.

Perhaps most challenging of all is critically engaging our own lenses—our assumptions, our actions, our way of doing life. Throughout the Gospel stories, that's what we see at the heart of discipleship. Whether it was the rich man who went away sad (Matthew 19), or the indignant self-righteousness of the older brother (Luke 15), or the exasperation of Martha (Luke 10), being confronted by the boundaries of our lenses and choosing to engage, rather than reject, our confusion and discomfort helps us to grow and go further as disciples of Jesus Christ. When we do this hard work, we are equipped with what we need to witness faithfully.

Witness Faithfully

Every Sunday at Urban Village, we practice the Christian tradition of giving testimony. For about five minutes, a community member gives others insight into her or his life. The stories range from unlikely friendships that pull us out of mental instability to a late-blooming relationship between an incarcerated father and young adult daughter to the experience of death and resurrection that accompanies one's transition from male to female.

The stories are as varied as the mind and imagination of God. They stretch the bounds of our individual experiences and drag the complexity of the rest of the world into what could otherwise devolve into an insular church culture. Many of these stories are an exercise in vulnerability as much as they are a performance of the ancient practice of witnessing to faith. They remind the community that God's house is indeed roomy, with enough space for all kinds of sojourners, on all kinds of journeys. This kind of reminder not only encourages the community internally but also empowers individuals to live their faith with authenticity, generosity, and inclusivity, knowing that God can be found in all kinds of places and people of this world. Dismantling Babylon's power involves dismantling walls of division and witnessing faithfully to God's inclusive love.

Be present. Invest joyfully. Engage critically. Witness faithfully. That's how we begin to disrupt Babylon.

Building an Anti-Racist Faith Community

While Urban Village Church, as a multi-site whole, is predominantly white, the particular congregation that I serve is more racially diverse. With outreach to the south side Chicago neighborhoods of Hyde Park and Woodlawn, our congregation is reflective of the area demographics, about half-and-half black and white. It might seem strange that an Asian American woman would find herself planting such a church—at least it did to me! But strange things can happen when you take the gospel seriously.

As I pastor a community of folks who come from diverse theological, socioeconomic, and educational backgrounds, I would say that the strongest gift I bring is the capacity to create a "container" where such diverse individuals can come together and grow to know one another authentically and intentionally. The practice of sharing testimony, described earlier, helps to break down initial assumptions that folks might hold: the quiet young woman who keeps to herself and seems a little too rigid is struggling to keep her head above the waters of anxiety and underemployment. The successful young doctor experiences God's constant companionship as he negotiates a low self-esteem that has bullied him from his childhood. The opportunities for vulnerable stories to be shared in a space that is not only safe and supportive but also one where the community journeys together, is foundational for trust and connection.

Disrupting Babylon is not a top-down enterprise. Top-down is how Babylon operates. The Christian tradition calls upon the community to engage from the ground up, building connections horizontally rather than vertically. And so, in a context where history has dictated that success is achieved through domination, subjugation, and colonization, the task of building Christian community involves engaging in practices that directly subvert those modes of engagement, eroding the power of Babylon.

Consciousness and Hospitality

Even while I might possess some requisite gifts, I've had to learn a lot about what it means to lead and learn from a congregation that not only embodies multiple layers of difference, but also how to partner meaningfully with colleagues whose contexts and identities are very different from my own. One of the guiding Scripture passages for me has been from 1 Corinthians 10:23-26 (CEB, adapted):

> Everything is permitted, but everything isn't beneficial. Everything is permitted, but everything doesn't build others up. No one should look out for their own advantage, but they should look out for each other. Eat everything that is

sold in the marketplace, without asking questions about it because of your conscience. *The earth and all that is in it belong to God.*

In other words, practice consciousness and hospitality.

Consciousness

There's this word in the passage translated as "conscience." Initially, when you think of a conscience, maybe you think of a little voice that helps you understand right from wrong. But the Greek word that Paul used, *syneidesis*, is deeper than that. It's more about a level of self-awareness. It is Consciousness with a capital C. Paul used this word to describe a deep and engaged thoughtfulness that underlies the decisions we make—particularly as people of faith. Paul was telling the Corinthians, in other words: Know yourself. God gave you a mind and a spirit that interact with each other *on purpose, for a purpose.* God wants you to be conscious—*aware*—of all that has shaped who you are, how others perceive you, and who you understand yourself to be.

Like most non-white immigrants, my mom wanted her children to grow up with the privileges that Whiteness afforded. She worked hard to hide herself from us. She didn't teach us to speak Chinese; we didn't observe any cultural holidays or markers of the year; she didn't even tell us stories from her childhood. She diminished herself to the greatest extent that she could so that our White side would dominate. It wasn't until much later in life—in seminary—that I came to understand how her diminishment of herself was all tied up in a system that encouraged this line of thinking.

I participated in a program that supported Asian American young adults in ministry formation. Having grown up in a predominantly white area and raised by a Chinese immigrant mother and white father, my understanding of critical race issues was significantly underdeveloped. I wouldn't have even called myself an

Asian American, a politically invented[5] term for the sake of consolidating power and building unity among the various Asian minorities in the United States.

I came to race consciousness because this program not only connected me with Asian American leaders in faith but also introduced questions and concepts that intersected with my identity in key ways. What does it mean to have a face like yours relegated to the status of perpetual foreigner—regardless of how many generations your family may have been in this country? ("Where are you from?" is the frequently encountered question.) How does the model minority[6] stereotype of Asian Americans intersect with, undergird, and contribute to anti-black racism in the United States? And, even more personally and painfully, what was it about US American society that led my mother to share her hopes that I would marry a white man so that her blood could be washed away? I could not overlook or ignore the fundamental sin that soaks these realities.

Questions such as these began to raise up within me a deeper inquiry of my own identity as a biracial woman negotiating the hyphens of categorization, and interstitial spaces of belonging, with increasing regularity. I began to sense that these questions were not only important for a greater understanding of my identity, but they were, in fact, central to shaping the vocational call I was moving toward. Realizing more and more the various ways that anti-Black racism functions in the United States as a fulcrum for White supremacy, I've discerned that the only way to dismantle this set-up is to refuse consistently and vigilantly to function as a lever for it—be it in the settings I choose to apply my gifts and skills for ministry, the shape of my leadership, or interpretations I make as a preacher of the gospel.

When creating spaces for anti-racist solidarity in diverse communities, I've learned that my capacity for a Christ-like Consciousness—the ability to know who I am and what I'm about—is key to developing honest relationships and true partnership. Because of my mother and the ways she chose to diminish herself, I have made a choice to call myself an Asian American and align myself as a person of color.

And so here I am, pastoring a congregation in which, for the most part, the only other Asian Americans are my partner and daughter. One of the gifts of growing up with parents of two different races and cultures is that you get a front-row seat to the miscommunications, misinterpretations, and dueling viewpoints that result from two such people trying to build a life together. As a result, if there is one skill I've developed, it's the capacity to hold loosely the many truths that exist among a group of individuals. I don't have the luxury of assuming that I know "my people" because, in a way, there is no "my people." Just because I have Consciousness, it doesn't mean my truth is the same as your truth. And so, this brings me to the second practice for building community: hospitality.

Hospitality

The first line of the passage is "Everything is permissible, but everything is not beneficial." But the second line is this: "Everything is permissible, but not everything builds others up." Just because I call myself a person of color doesn't mean I don't benefit from the system. I don't get pulled over when I drive in certain neighborhoods, I don't speak with an accent, and people don't ask about my citizenship.

And so, I hold my truth and experiences in tension with the truths and experiences of those around me. Being in authentic community with others means being committed to one another, even when our truths collide. If I have really done my Consciousness work, it will be paired with an ego that is strong enough, and a spirit of hospitality that is sincere enough, to step aside and let go of my "rights" so that others might also have space. Rather than being race traitors, betraying the tribal bounds of race, power, and privilege, Christians are called to be catalysts for new ways of doing community, refusing to play by Babylon's rules and choosing instead to engage in an alternative rule of life, kin-dom practices.

The outcome of this kind of hospitality is not self-diminishment but rather *gracious mutuality*: creating space for multiple truths to be shared, engaged, and understood for the sake of deeper community and a more robust experience of God's kin-dom. While Consciousness helps us assert who we are, when we have worked through the grief and complexity of the questions, we are freed up internally to offer generous hospitality externally: an orientation of who I am (Consciousness) paired with a spaciousness for all of who you are (Hospitality).

This, of course, is lifelong work. Sometimes we get it right and sometimes we get it disastrously wrong. But we try, and we keep trying. Because this is the pilgrimage of discipleship and because this is what it means to be the kin-dom of God.

And this is how we begin to disrupt Babylon.

Notes

1. More on this later.

2. Hawaiian term, initially used to describe the children of Caucasian (*haole*) and Hawaiian parents but commonly used to describe persons of mixed Caucasian and Asian makeup.

3. Sometimes you will find that I have capitalized the word *White* while other times it is not. This is to differentiate between "white" as a descriptor and "White" as a politically constructed identity in the US context, not unlike the difference between "black" and "Black."

4. Not all that different from micro aggressions, these are the well-intentioned assumptions of good, kind people who assume and gently enforce what constitutes norms of culture and experience, ranging from history to standards of beauty to acceptable forms of communication.

5. The term "Asian American" was coined by historian Yuji Ichioka, who is credited with popularizing the term to frame a new "inter-ethnic-pan-Asian American self-defining political group" in the late 1960s.

6. The term "model minority" was widely introduced during the mid-1960s and was used to highlight the achievements of Asian Americans over and against those of non-White US Americans. This label served as a vehicle for reinforcing racial hierarchies based on income, education, crime statistics, and family stability. Many would argue that this is a positive stereotype, but in reality it only serves to further divide minority groups and silence Asian Americans while reinforcing a low-level sense of threat of Asian Americans to White success.

CHAPTER 4

Building Intercultural Churches with the End in Sight

Rev. Dr. Curtiss Paul DeYoung

The vision of heavenly oneness in Revelation 7 has engaged follow-ers of Jesus through the centuries in the pursuit of reconciliation and unity in their earthly realities. The Revelator proclaims that our end is in sight. When building intercultural churches, we keep this vision as our end goal. In order to arrive at this desired end of such broadly inclusive congregations, cultural competency and deconstruction of power differentials become of the utmost impor-tance. Our challenge is to develop transformational leaders who can implement such change.

My perspective about intercultural churches is informed by my personal journey, the biblical narrative, and United States history. So I begin with an overview of what I have discovered and how my understanding has grown from my own research of intercultural congregations as a scholar and participant. I draw upon my work in *United by Faith*[1] and *Radical Reconciliation*,[2] as well as my direct engagement with intercultural congregations in the United States and in South Africa.

My Journey . . . A Glimpse of the End in Sight

My experience of church life began in monocultural congrega-tions attended by whites like me. My father was a pastor in the Church of God (Anderson, Indiana), and his congregations were located in suburbs and rural areas populated by whites in the United States. There was one exception. For a brief moment during my preschool years in the early 1960s, my father pastored a racially diverse congregation in Dowagiac, Michigan. I do not have memories of this. But it changed the way my parents thought about race issues in the United States.

It was not until I moved to New York City after graduation from college in 1981 that I had a significant church experience outside of my own racial ethnic culture. I began attending the all-black Congregational Church of God in Harlem. Pastor Rev. Levorn Aaron took me under his wing and mentored me as his apprentice in ministry. For a year I worshiped and learned to preach in this Southern-flavored urban African American church.

After a year in New York City I moved to Anderson, Indiana, to attend the Church of God seminary. My world had been altered, and I could no longer attend a predominantly white congregation. So I began attending Arrow Heights Church of God. This intercultural congregation was a mix of African Americans, older whites (from the time the congregation was all white), and college and seminary students who were often white. The congregation was active in addressing the issues of its economically impoverished neighbors and members.

In 1983, I moved to Washington, DC, to serve as a ministerial intern with Rev. Dr. Samuel Hines at Third Street Church of God. The congregation was mostly black but intercultural, nearly evenly divided between African Americans and immigrants from the West Indies.

In January 1986, after graduation from seminary, my wife and I moved to Minneapolis, Minnesota, where I became senior pastor of First Church of God. This congregation was in a neighborhood that was transitioning from a white neighborhood to a multicultural neighborhood. I stayed at the church nearly five years as the congregation went from being 95 percent white to 30 percent persons of color (Hmong and African American).

I left First Church of God in 1990 and began work in nonprofit and academic sectors. My family decided to attend Park Avenue United Methodist Church, a congregation that embraced an intercultural identity in the late 1960s. The congregation's demographics typically have been about 60 percent white, 35 percent African American, and 5 percent Latino. The pastoral staff is diverse.

After cowriting *United by Faith* in 2003, I began to get invitations to visit, speak at, or consult with various diverse congregations. Among those that I have had extended relationships with and learned from are congregations from Pasadena to Minneapolis to New York.

The Biblical Narrative . . . with the End in Sight

My journey has been deeply informed by the biblical narrative.[3] The story of intercultural churches began with Christianity's first congregation in Jerusalem, which emerged from Jesus' Galilean followers. On the day of Pentecost the power of the Holy Spirit came upon 120 Galileans praying in an upper room. They ran into the streets proclaiming the good news of Jesus Christ in the languages of the nations. People from Jewish enclaves on the continents of Asia, Africa, and Europe who had immigrated to Jerusalem heard the gospel in the local dialect of their community in the country of their origin. (Acts 2:5, NRSV). As a result, a congregation of thousands of intercultural, multilingual Jews was established in Jerusalem (Acts 2:41). The church was intercultural and multilingual from its inception.

This diverse Jerusalem congregation operated at the margins of Judaism because second-class Galilean Jews and migrant Hellenized Jews were the core membership. Later on mainstream Jews of Jerusalem joined the congregation as "a great many of the priests became obedient to the faith" (Acts 6:7, NRSV).

Acts and the letters of the apostle Paul proclaim a narrative of a first-century church whose congregations from Jerusalem to Antioch to Rome were inclusive of a wide range of ethnic backgrounds and cultural perspectives. According to Acts, the first congregation where Jews and Greeks blended into one faith community was in Antioch of Syria. As the third largest city in the Roman Empire, Antioch was inhabited by a wide cultural mix of peoples. There were ethnic tensions in the city with mobs attacking Jews and setting fire to their synagogues.

Many Greek-speaking Jewish Christians left Jerusalem because of persecution and traveled to Antioch. They reached out to fellow Jews (Acts 11:19). Then some of their Cyrenean and Cypriot leaders also engaged Greeks (11:20). Barnabas was sent by the Jerusalem church to provide leadership and a link with the mother church (11:24). Saul of Tarsus, later known as the apostle Paul, joined the leadership team (11:25-26). Both Paul and Barnabas were raised in Jewish communities outside of Palestine but also immersed in Greek culture. They were bilingual, speaking Aramaic and Greek. Three others were leaders: Manean was raised as a stepbrother of Herod Antipas; Lucius of Cyrene was from North Africa; Simeon was called Niger (black), therefore he most likely was a black African (13:1). This group of leaders had the necessary cultural competency required for diverse Antioch.

Jews and Gentiles in the Antioch congregation continued to embrace their culture of origin. But they also set aside certain cultural rules that blocked their ability to practice a communal life such as eating and socializing together. While this was not typically allowed, in "the many house-congregations of Antioch . . . Jews and Gentiles, living together in crowded city quarters, freely mixed."[4] In the midst of Antioch's extreme ethnic tensions "Christianity offered a new basis for social solidarity."[5]

Most of the congregations in the first century, including the church at Antioch, were formed in the shadow of the colonial Roman Empire. Congregations were a diverse mix of colonized persons and those who were colonizers or beneficiaries of colonization. Colonized Jews worshiping and fellowshiping with Romans and Greeks exposed the power differentials in society. In the midst of Roman colonial realities these intercultural congregations were formed by oppressed ethnic minority Jews who welcomed dominant-culture Romans and Greeks into their churches under the leadership of Jews. Therefore, the primary biblical model of a Christian congregation was intercultural and one where members of an oppressed minority community welcomed people from the privileged dominant culture into the local church.

United States History . . . Lost Without the End in Sight

While the biblical account seems to point clearly to intercultural congregations as the primary model, the church in the United States tells a different story.[6] The church that arrived in what would become the United States was transported from Europe as part of the colonial enterprise and participated in the genocide of Native Americans and the enslavement of Africans. A divided and racist church was planted in the spiritual soil of what became the United States; this church contradicted the reality of the first-century intercultural church and the vision of Revelation 7. The model of church as racially and culturally segregated was built on the foundation of white supremacy.

Native Americans who embraced Christianity were separated by European settlers into a number of segregated towns of "praying Indians." These specially created villages housed Christian Native Americans in order to isolate them from American Indians practicing traditional religions and from white Christians. Blacks were invited into churches with whites, but they were assigned separate seating called the "Negro pew." Also, many pastors owned enslaved Africans, who were sometimes included along with the furniture for the parsonage.

In the mid-1700s, the Great Awakening revival movement spread across the United States, and many poor whites and enslaved Africans came into the Christian faith. Sociologist C. Eric Lincoln noted, "What the Africans found in the camp meetings of the Great Awakening was *acceptance and involvement as human beings.*"[7] Some intercultural congregations of whites and African Americans emerged out of the Great Awakening. Poor whites who did not own slaves primarily populated these intercultural congregations, which "enabled them to see blacks as potential fellow believers in a way that white worshipers in more elite churches seldom could."[8]

What historian Paul Harvey wrote about the Southern Baptists provides insight into why these intercultural congregations were short in duration: "Southern Baptists never accepted their African American coreligionists as equals. They lacked the will, the fortitude, the theology, and the intellectual tools to even contemplate doing so."[9]

Where possible, African Americans also developed parallel opportunities for worship and fellowship. Enslaved persons of African descent created their own unique forms of Christian interpretation and practice that spoke to the conditions created by racism and contained cultural patterns retained from their origins in various parts of the African continent. Hidden away from the view of the slaveholder, African Americans formed their own churches. These invisible institutions[10] laid the foundations for African American congregations and denominations.

Free blacks in the North departed from white churches to start their own congregations and denominations as early as 1787. By the early 1800s these had formalized into new denominations such as the African Methodist Episcopal Church (1816) and the African Methodist Episcopal Zion Church (1820). As the Civil War ended, African Americans left white denominations and congregations where they sat in Negro pews, causing the accelerated formation of black congregations and denominations.

There were a few attempts made in the years after the Civil War to cross the racial divide in US Christianity. In the early 1880s a group currently identified as the Church of God (Anderson, Indiana) defied segregation laws in the South by holding interracial worship events and in the North established several intercultural congregations. Shortly after the turn of the century, the Church of God's practice of racial inclusiveness mostly disappeared.

Another brief emergence of intercultural Christianity occurred in 1906 in Los Angeles, California. An African American ordained minister of the Church of God (Anderson, Indiana) named William Seymour was central to what many have called the birth of the modern Pentecostal movement. The Azusa Street Revival was promising in its diversity with African Americans and whites attending in similar numbers and the presence of Latinos, Asian Americans, and Native Americans. Seymour intentionally enlisted people of all races, including women, to serve in leadership. The Azusa Street Revival ended in 1909. Racism played a significant role in its demise. Several Pentecostal denominations that emerged from the Azusa Street Revival began as interracial groups, yet all split by race within a few years.

What happened to the faith of first-century churches that could produce intercultural congregations? Church historian Lester B. Scherer writes: "The same defect of imagination that made it possible to enslave Africans in the first place made it virtually impossible for whites to envision them as authentic co-members of any community, including a Christian congregation. . . . Christian fellowship stopped at the color line."[11] In the United States the church became a principal divider of people by race and culture. Perhaps sociologist W. E. B. Du Bois was right when he wrote in 1929, "The American Church of Christ is Jim Crowed from top to bottom. No other institution in America is built so thoroughly or more absolutely on the color line. Everybody knows this."[12]

Components of an Intercultural Church

Through my study of intercultural churches as a scholar and a participant, I have come to the conclusion that in order for intercultural congregations to represent a Revelation 7 vision, they must exhibit cultural competency and deconstruct power differentials. While the descriptions of first-century biblical congregations support this premise, the inability to create and sustain intercultural congregations throughout US history reveals a deficiency in modern-day approaches.

Both Pentecost and the vision of Revelation 7—the beginning and the end of the church—exemplify a proactive cultural competency and deconstruction of power differentials. At the end in Revelation, the church gathers around the heavenly throne fully inhabiting their specific cultural identities and representing a full acceptance and understanding of each other's culture. Meanwhile the Revelator's cadence of nations, tribes, peoples, and languages occurs several times in Revelation, and each time it is stated in a new order illustrating the equality represented when no one group dominates. Pentecost also reveals the cultural competency and deconstructing power dynamics in the early church, as we shall see.

Cultural Competency

Pentecost established the inherent intercultural nature of the biblical church and hints at a kind of cultural competency. Biblical scholar Virginia Burrus remarks about Pentecost that "the disciples find not their own but 'other' hot languages in their mouths."[13] When the Holy Spirit descended upon them at Pentecost, the disciples opened their mouths and someone else's language came out. Yet at the same time these disciples were still their own cultural selves. They spoke these other languages with their Galilean accents still intact. "Are not all these who are speaking Galileans?" (Acts 2:7, NRSV). Cultural competency is understanding deeply the experience of another while still being rooted in your own cultural reality.

How do we learn to speak the language of other people's experience? The Pentecost text reminds us that the wind was heard before "a tongue rested on each of them" (Acts 2:3, NRSV). Hearing preceded speaking. Cultural competency requires that we listen to stories and observe ways of living. Intercultural pastor Jacqueline

Lewis writes that leaders of intercultural congregations "need the capacity to be multivocal; they must speak in tongues."[14] Multivocal capacity comes from deep intentional listening.

After taking several courses at Howard University School of Divinity, I had become conversant in black liberation theology. I remember having a conversation with Dr. Samuel Hines, my pastor. At the time he was not convinced about black theology. As a white man raised in white suburbs, I was arguing for black theology while my black pastor was arguing against it. The words I was saying were those of my Howard University professors. It was as though another language came out of my mouth! The language did not match my background or my look. It was a Pentecost moment. It represented a growing competency in the ways of thinking and understanding in my new social location.

Another way to envision cultural competency is through intercultural worship. In my first visit to South Africa in 2000, I attended one of those unique moments in South Africa where people worshiped together across racial and cultural lines. The worship experience merged indigenous African musical forms with elements of Europe and even traces from the United States. The diversity in language, culture, style, and expression was expansive and moving. The worship leaders sang in multiple languages while blending diverse cultural musical genres. It was a virtual symphony of cultural competency.

Intercultural congregations can create an in-between space, a third place, a hybrid reality where cultures resonate, interact, and blend with each other. This creolizing effect produces a deeper level of shared cultural competency. I visited the French Caribbean island of Guadeloupe a few years ago. Since I do not speak French, I was dependent on a translator. On Sunday we attended church, and I asked my translator to tell me when people spoke French and when they spoke Creole. After a church member finished praying, my translator noted that the prayer began in French and ended in Creole. I asked why the person used two languages in prayer. My translator informed me that French was used to speak of the majesty of God. But Creole was used when speaking more personally of suffering and struggles. Creole was the language of the heart.

At Pentecost "each one heard them speaking in the native language of each. . . . 'How is it that we hear, each of us, in our own native language?'" (Acts 2:6,8, NRSV). Hearing in your own particular dialect of your native language is a powerful experience. We discover cultural competency when we learn to listen to and speak in the language of each other's hearts.

The gap in cultural understanding and lived experience between whites and persons of color is one of the greatest challenges for intercultural congregations. Persons of color often live and work in a world dominated by white cultural ways, so they know much about whites. Few whites have a deep knowledge of other cultures or have experience that creates an understanding of racism and prejudice. Members of intercultural congregations must discover ways to become culturally fluent in the experience of others.[15]

Deconstructing Power

A second feature I want to identify in first-century congregations is how power was deconstructed.[16] We see it first in how the Holy Spirit moved through multiple Pentecost events. On the day of Pentecost in Jerusalem, the Spirit created an inclusive equality between Galilean Jews and Diasporic Jews (Acts 2). When the Spirit visited Samaria an inclusive equality was established between Samaritans and Jews (Acts 8). Then when the Spirit came to the home of the Roman centurion Cornelius, Jews and Romans were brought into an equal fellowship (Acts 10). The Pentecosts, particularly in Acts 2, also pronounce inclusive equality across the power divide expressed in generation, gender, and class. The Holy Spirit deconstructs power and privilege.

This process of addressing power manifested in the new congregations. First-century intercultural churches were small, Jewish, home-based congregations where Romans and Greeks entered these Jewish homes as guests and as equals. As Romans and Greeks joined with oppressed Jews, their privileged perspectives and positions had to be discarded. Biblical scholar Tat-siong Benny Liew calls this "status inversion."[17] When Romans and Greeks joined Jewish congregations, they became identified with a socially stigmatized people and became family with a marginalized community. The fact that Jews were leaders in first-generation churches was another way that status inversion occurred. Once again empire privileges did not function in the church.

As we saw in the history of church in the United States, modern congregations have been formed using models from the womb of privilege. Even intercultural churches have been influenced by this history and often operate like dominant culture churches. Too often the church reflects a white, male, middle-class, able-bodied, heterosexual, exclusive viewpoint. Counter to first-century church realities, intercultural congregations today often invite persons of color into privilege rather than asking whites to discard racial privileges. Assimilation into dominant culture is the result. To be authentically intercultural, congregations must dismantle the power and privilege differentials imposed by society through a radical status inversion that creates a truly reconciled community of faith.

Developing Leaders . . . with the End in Sight

Developing leaders with a Revelation 7 vision as the end in sight is essential for intercultural churches. Seminary professor and author Soong-Chan Rah states, "If you are a white Christian wanting to be a missionary in this day and age, and you have never had a nonwhite mentor, then you will not be a missionary. You will be colonialist. Instead of taking the gospel message into the world, you will take an Americanized version of the gospel."[18] I paraphrase Rah and say if you are a dominant-culture person wanting to provide leadership in an intercultural congregation, and you have never had a mentor of another culture or race, you will be a colonialist reproducing a dominant-culture version of the church.

Intercultural church leaders must be equipped in cultural understanding and nuance and be able to think critically in order to create congregational environments where privilege and power are deconstructed. The first-century church had the same challenges in their congregations. As a marginalized community in the Roman Empire, Jews understood the ways of the dominant group in order to survive. For Greeks and Romans to fully reconcile with Jews, they had to learn firsthand the effects of marginalization from those who understood it best. Paul mentored Romans and Greeks side by side with Jews he was developing into leaders (Colossians 4:7-17).

The ultimate goal for intercultural churches is a leadership representative of all cultures, each of whom is fluent in other cultures and has a social justice framework for shaping the congregation. Dominant-culture whites in the United States need to be mentored for leadership by persons from other cultures who have direct experience with the impact of oppression so as to gain both a cultural lens and a power/privilege lens. Perhaps all seminarians should be required to have an apprenticeship in a congregation where the leaders are different from their culture of origin.

A Pentecost-infused Revelation 7 vision of the end in sight produces congregations that are intercultural through cultural competency and deconstructing power differentials. While this chapter has focused on racial and ethnic culture, this same vision and process applies to diversity in gender, class, sexual orientation, ability, and the like. In order for congregations to become intercultural, they must address all places of alienation, marginalization, and injustice and build faith communities that are fully inclusive and radically just.

Notes

1. Curtiss Paul DeYoung, Michael O. Emerson, George Yancey, and Karen Chai Kim, *United by Faith: The Multiracial Congregation as an Answer to the Problem of Race* (New York: Oxford University Press, 2003).

2. Allan Aubrey Boesak and Curtiss Paul DeYoung, *Radical Reconciliation: Beyond Political Pietism and Christian Quietism* (Maryknoll, NY: Orbis Books, 2012).

3. This section uses information found in DeYoung et al., *United by Faith*, 21–37, and Boesak and DeYoung, *Radical Reconciliation*, 79–85.

4. Richard A. Horsley and Neil Asher Silberman, *The Message and Kingdom: How Jesus and Paul Ignited a Revolution and Transformed the Ancient World* (New York: Grosset/Putnam, 1997), 142.

5. Rodney Stark, *The Rise of Christianity: A Sociologist Reconsiders History* (Princeton, NJ: Princeton University Press, 1996), 161.

6. This section uses information found in DeYoung et al., *United by Faith*, 41–61.

7. C. Eric Lincoln, *Race, Religion, and the Continuing American Dilemma* (New York: Hill and Wang, 1999), 48.

8. John B. Boles, ed., *Masters and Slaves in the House of the Lord: Race and Religion in the American South, 1740–1870* (Lexington: University Press of Kentucky, 1988), 9.

9. Paul Harvey, *Redeeming the South: Religious Cultures and Racial Identities among Southern Baptists 1865–1925* (Chapel Hill: University of North Carolina Press, 1997), 9.

10. E. Franklin Frazier, *The Negro Church in America* (New York: Schocken, 1974), 23–25.

11. Lester B. Scherer, *Slavery and the Churches in Early America 1619-1819* (Grand Rapids, MI: Eerdmans, 1975), 154–55, 156–57.

12. W. E. B. Du Bois, "The Color Line and the Church," in *Du Bois on Religion*, ed. Phil Zuckerman (Walnut Creek, CA: AltaMira Press, 2000), 169.

13. Virginia Burrus, "The Gospel of Luke and the Acts of the Apostles," in *A Postcolonial Commentary on the New Testament Writings*, ed. Fernando F. Segovia and R. S. Sugirtharajah (London: T & T Clark, 2009), 147.

14. Lewis, *Power of Stories*, 68.

15. For more on multicultural fluency, see Curtiss Paul DeYoung, *Coming Together in the Twenty-first Century: The Bible's Message in an Age of Diversity* (Valley Forge, PA: Judson Press, 2009), 167–70.

16. This section uses information found in Boesak and DeYoung, *Radical Reconciliation*, 79–90.

17. Tat-siong Benny Liew, "Redressing Bodies in Corinth: Racial/Ethnic Politics and Religious Difference in the Context of Empire," in *The Colonized Apostle: Paul through Postcolonial Eyes*, ed. Christopher D. Stanley (Minneapolis: Fortress, 2011), 133.

18. Soong-Chan Rah, *The Next Evangelicalism: Freeing the Church from Western Cultural Captivity* (Downers Grove, IL: IVP Books, 2009), 162.

CHAPTER 5

Embodying a Disruptive Journey

Rev. Carlos Ruiz

One morning at our church, I gave an announcement inviting people to volunteer in the ministry of teaching ESL (English as a Second Language). I described my experience serving with immigrants from different places in South America and encouraged church members to consider serving in this intercultural ministry, telling them how fun and rewarding that would be. I sat down and continued with my day, my week, and my pastoral responsibilities. A week later I got a call from Jorge,[1] a student in the church ESL program and an attendee at the church. He wanted to talk. I happily agreed to meet, and we set a time and a day.

As we greeted each other and began to talk, Jorge shared how he was very hurt by me. I couldn't understand because I didn't remember anything that I had done to upset him. However, I asked him what I had done that hurt him so badly. I saw his eyes fill with tears between deep sadness and fear. He immediately responded that it was the jovial way I had given the announcement the previous week at church that had hurt him. I sat confused, shocked, and worried because I still couldn't connect the dots.

In the meantime, Jorge sat in front of me, beginning to sweat profusely, and his face looked as if he were in a panic. I immediately tried to create an environment where he could feel safe and told him it was okay to feel what he was feeling, but still I was shocked and not understanding what was occurring.

* * *

On another occasion in a fellowship event our congregation attempted to create a space for people of different ethnic groups and cultures where we could talk about our differences and move toward reconciliation. Our hope and our prayer was that perhaps we would learn to listen to one another so that we could grow closer together toward the *shalom* of our community. Little by little the conversation had escalated that day, and the pain of some people of color came to the surface. Some people raised their voices, and someone burst into crying, saying she couldn't take some of the white people's insensitivity any longer. The white person who was standing said he wanted to understand and learn how to listen better; the person of color replied that it wasn't worth it, as if the white man had insulted her deeply. She went out of the room crying and screaming. Several people went out to follow her, feeling shocked and perplexed by her abrupt and powerful reaction.

Pursuing a Ministry of Reconciliation

These two stories are examples of the many situations and encounters we often witness in our multi-ethnic context. Everything begins with a noble and sincere desire to follow the gospel of Jesus Christ and live out the reconciliation of all people. At some point, however, that good beginning seems to turn into painful feelings of panic, helplessness, and rage, leaving us as leaders discouraged and not knowing exactly what occurred and how to respond.

We are a people who believe that living in a segregated and broken context is not the last word or the story we want to live. The gospel of Jesus helps us to imagine a story not where we all continue living lives that are segregated, but a story where reconciliation between people who have caused unspeakable violence to each other takes place. However, many times the pain that comes to the surface is unbearable, such that reactions between people who are different seem to be erratic, volatile, and even violent.

If we understand the reconciliation of all people as the process of mending relationships after great injuries have been committed, what do we do when the pain that these injuries caused seems to linger longer and longer? What do we do when things that occurred in the past continue to come alive as if we are experiencing them again and again? What do we do when the word *reconciliation* causes panic, hopelessness, helplessness, or outright rage in people who have suffered unspeakable brutality, as is the case of many black and brown people in our society?

After engaging in the work of reconciliation for more than a decade as a pastor and as a psychotherapist, I am convinced that the very process of engaging in reconciliation carries in itself deep injury and more specifically trauma. As theologian Shelley Rambo wisely writes in *Spirit and Trauma*: "Trauma is the key to articulating a theology of redemption rather than the problem around which theology must navigate."[2] I will add that this is also true about reconciliation as it is understood and practiced in the milieu of broken relationships perpetuated by racism and injustice.

Trauma provides a set of lenses so that we can experience what the apostle Paul described as God reconciling people through Christ. The main ministry entrusted to us as Jesus' followers is the ministry of reconciliation (see 2 Corinthians 5:18-20). Our mission is to restore by the power of the Spirit what has been broken or divided. However, how are we supposed to do that when the injury we are trying to mend seems to linger in our bodies and in our psyches in the form of overwhelming panic, terror, numbness, rage, and helplessness?

In this chapter, I will look at reconciliation as a core value that is central to the gospel of Jesus Christ, and I will explore how the lens that trauma gives us is central in order to understand the work of reconciliation as a hopeful journey toward *shalom*.

At the same time, I will argue for a different understanding of reconciliation. I will explore how the journey of reconciliation always includes trauma where the categories of life and death are not so clearly delineated, not knowing exactly where life ends and death begins but how they coexist in the journey of the person and communities. This different understanding does not allow us to imagine reconciliation in a linear way but in a cyclical manner. And we discover where the work of the Spirit occurs, in the words of Rambo, "in the middle,"[3] where everything seems still unfinished, still broken, and where pain and the effects of violence linger.

The Nature and Effects of Trauma

By "trauma" I mean the original meaning of the word,[4] that is, a deep wound in a person's psyche, soul, mind, and body due to a tragic, violent, overwhelming, perceived, or real event. This wound is so destabilizing and pervasive that it continues affecting the person's mind and body even if the event had occurred a long time ago. That is because there are parts of us that have been traumatized and continue experiencing the violence and the suffering as if it were still occurring. In other words, experiencing trauma is not merely remembering the horrific or overwhelming events we experienced but reliving them.

Trauma poses a problem in many people's lives long after the traumatic events occurred. How does reconciliation get lived out when the injury that we are trying to address continues to be re-experienced in people's bodies, even if the intention of change and not repeating the injury is there? Trauma defies time. No wonder explosions of anger, rage, or panic that seem disproportionate occur in many of the ethnic and racial reconciliation conversations and encounters we have had in our communities and churches. While trauma is what happened in the past and continues possessing people in the present, for many the realities of discrimination, racism, brutality, and violence continue occurring as their everyday circumstances.

Rambo writes, "Trauma is what does not go away. It persists in symptoms that live on in the body, in the intrusive fragments of memories that return. It persists in symptoms that live on in communities, in the layers of past violence that constitute present ways of relating."[5] Pursuing reconciliation in the context of trauma can be one of the most humbling and disorienting paths. Trying to amend past violence as if it were just "a past" will continually confront us with the way the present ways of relating are informed and caused by that "past violence" that continues being experienced as an insidious present that won't go away.

The effects of experiencing trauma are legion. However, I will focus on just one in this chapter. One of the characteristics in the aftermath of trauma is the disorganization of the imagination. This disorganization affects the ability of trauma-affected people to tell stories that are life-giving and hopeful about themselves and their world.

Theologian Serene Jones writes in *Trauma and Grace*: "I use the word imagination to refer to the fact that as human beings we constantly engage the world through organizing stories, or habits of mind, which structure our thoughts".[6]

This means that when people experience violence, and their souls and bodies go through trauma, as in the case of racism and poverty, this capacity to organize stories that lead to flourishing is harmed and at times deeply wounded. The result is that individuals and communities internalize that unresolved sense of terror and being unable to resolve it, they replay it in their bodies in the form of rage, panic, helplessness, or paralysis. These feelings provoke a sense of despair and an inability to imagine a future where human flourishing can happen.

This could have disastrous consequences when the idea of reconciliation is presented to ethnic minority people who have suffered trauma related to their minority identity. Essentially, reconciliation is a return to the flourishing of human relationships. It is impossible for those who have suffered trauma to conceive of being reconciled when the injury and the pain of the injury continue reoccurring in their body and psyche.

When we consider that trauma affects the way we envision the future of our stories, if the story is one of failure and despair, it can affect the way we set goals, making persons who have suffered violence unable to imagine and experience any goal they would want to reach. This inability to set goals carries through life as the person continues to devalue any sense of hope, agency, or power to control his or her circumstances. If trauma affects the way we know and see the world, it makes us ask, "How are we, communities that pursue reconciliation, to think theologically about reconciliation, taking into account the pernicious effects of trauma?"

Doing Theology from the Middle

If trauma reconfigures the way we experience and understand time, it will challenge traditional ways of understanding and engaging stories. This means that one of the things we will have to view through different lenses will be the critical events in the Christian story. According to Rambo, one aspect of Christian theology that remains unexplored is the narrative of death and life. Death and life have been understood by some theologians as linear categories. The lenses of trauma, however, will certainly make us see differently the traditional categories of death and life, particularly as they are narrated in the events of cross and resurrection. Rambo explains that trauma makes us look at and experience the neat and clear-cut categories of death and life, turning our attention to a more mixed terrain of remaining, one that she identifies as the "middle."[7] Therefore trauma has the possibility of bearing fruit by transforming a simplistic worldview into one that is more nuanced, more complex, more helpful in real, lived experience.

This terrain of the middle doesn't let us look at death and life as if they are opposed to each other. On the contrary, it helps us to imagine that death is not the absence of life and that life is not untouched by the reality of death. Death and life belong to each other and coexist in the narrative we all live, and particularly in trauma. This way of understanding helps us to imagine and do theology where reconciliation occurs in the middle, in the unfinished and still broken places that don't seem to heal easily.

In reflecting about the relationship between death and life in the Scriptures, philosopher Peter Rollins writes in *The Divine Magician*: "In the story of Adam and Eve we witness the description of a death that operates *within* life, a death that is manifested in this incessant inner drive that causes us to act against ourselves."[8] In this passage Rollins identifies that death and life in Scripture are not as separated from each other as we normally think, but there is a death that operates *within* life that makes it hard to know when one starts and the other ends.

In the case of the stories I narrated above, I created an extreme sense of danger for Jorge by my impulse to move so quickly to the reward and "joy" of being reconciled without staying in the middle with the pain. This produced a physical reaction and a severe sense of panic so that all he wanted at the moment was to escape. My linear understanding of reconciliation didn't make a space for the suffering he carried that didn't seem to go away. Later on, during our conversation I learned of the horrific violence and terror he had experienced as he crossed the border from Mexico to the United States. He narrated how he witnessed the rapes of his friends and the brutality against the people he crossed with and that he could not escape or erase these events from his mind. My naïve and jovial tone as I gave the announcement that morning not only didn't match the gravity of his traumatic context and experiences but also, as he told me that day, didn't make him feel safe or have any feeling of solidarity on my part, thus causing him to feel alone at church that day. It triggered the violence of "the past" that he experienced in the present.

In the same way, in the second situation I narrated above, the woman who exploded in rage and hurt did so because she was reliving the humiliations and violence her parents had suffered as victims of racism and discrimination when she was a child. The comment of the white person who said he wanted to understand sounded like an utter minimization and trivialization of her pain, which occurred in the past but was still part of her present. The implication that her memories of the violence her parents had experienced were abstract information for "understanding" or an exercise in "learning how to listen" made her present pain emerge with full force without being able to escape. Comments like that created a sense of profound danger for her as well. She couldn't make fit the violence and rage she continued re-experiencing with the sincere comment made by the white man that revealed his unexplored guilt and shame, wanting to gloss over the death and get to the life so quickly.

Having reflected on these stories, I know that reconciliation in the church needs to be imagined and lived out from the middle and not in a linear manner where death and life are separated from each other. It is necessary that the unfinished, broken middle space be witnessed in order to see glimpses of new life and healing. Understandings of reconciliation that move too quickly from death to life are tremendously naïve, failing to witness the trauma that doesn't go away, that still remains.

For those of us who have the deep longing and calling for imagining and creating healthy communities where the gospel of Jesus Christ guides us toward wholeness and reconciliation, the natural question that emerges is: How are we to embody and move toward reconciliation and healing in view of the prevalence and presence of historic and personal trauma in our communities? What is the alternative of healing when we inhabit the middle space?

Toward Healing

It would be easy to conclude that trauma leaves us hopeless and perpetuating a story of despair when it comes to the call of the gospel to reconciliation and *shalom* building. However, the opposite is true. The experience of trauma, with all its devastating consequences to people, can become a creative wellspring when we allow ourselves to witness people's stories of violence that dwell in the middle space.

A biblical story that has been helpful to me as a paradigm of healing from the middle space is found in Numbers 21. The Israelites were in the wilderness and had sinned against God. After this, serpents came out and bit them, leaving many Israelites dead in the desert. They must have experienced a traumatic terror as they saw friends and family being attacked and dying by the frightening serpents. After they repented of their sin and asked God for help, it would have made sense for God to remove the serpents right away in order to heal them. On the contrary, God asked Moses to build an icon of the very creature that was causing them to die, a serpent of bronze. Whenever they would look at the serpent of bronze, they would be healed and live.

I am *not* suggesting that trauma comes because we sinned, as in this biblical story, but I do think the story could offer a paradigm to pursue healing through the lens of trauma and from the middle.

In this story God tells Moses that the people need to look at the figure of the snake of bronze so that they could be healed and live. What an odd way of being saved![9] If they looked at the traumatic icon instead of running away from it, they would live. I cannot imagine what the Israelites felt when Moses told them that.

This story reminds me that many serpents have bitten us in this life, injecting us with some of their poison in the form of trauma and death. This poison has shattered what we knew as life, introducing us into a different kind of life/death where panic, rage, and hopelessness don't go away. When I think about this story, I understand that similar situations are occurring in our communities today. There is in all of us, especially in environments where we want to pursue and experience reconciliation, a big desire to move on and not look at the snakes that have come out to bite and kill for generations. We feel afraid and helpless, and we are ashamed of the little "progress" we have made to the point that we want to push harder or disengage. The story of the serpent of bronze doesn't let us choose either of those options; on the contrary, it tells us that we need to look at our own serpent of bronze if we want to embrace healing and live. The same trauma we suffer and want to escape from is the very trauma we need to look at.

We cannot look at our serpent of bronze and live without experiencing the counterintuitive and frightening feeling of diving into what can be unfinished and deeply marred in our stories. We cannot look at our trauma or the trauma of others without embodying in our communities the practice of witnessing. Just as the Israelites looked at the serpent of bronze and lived, so we are called to witness the trauma of others and the suffering that remains.

It is crucial, as we engage in the work of reconciliation, that we become safe and compassionate communities and churches where we can serve and minister with people who have suffered trauma. The ministry of the Holy Spirit happens not by moving fast through the places of pain and heartache but by witnessing the middle where all still remains broken and where the violence is part of the present. The story of the serpent of bronze becomes paradigmatic because in looking at our traumas and witnessing the suffering that remains, we create by God's grace a space where others can be seen and receive life and flourish.

Witnessing with others the middle space makes room for the unconcluded suffering that continues to repeat itself. Witnessing brings the presence that affirms and sees with compassion what the other is still replaying. Witnessing then expands and creates space for death and life to coexist as people who have suffered trauma narrate the stories of horror and violence they have suffered. In the work of reconciliation, we need to become aware of the healing and almost imperceptible presence of the Holy Spirit by witnessing the suffering that hasn't been put into words or story form.

It is in that space where the Spirit shines like a constant blue flame and groans with people with unspeakable groans (Romans 8:26) where the death that was suffered returns in order to be reintegrated in the life story of the person. This return creates a cohesive story where the traumatic event becomes finally part of the life story of the person, opening the door to new possibilities. Witnessing creates space where God's love and grace can be accessed. Because of God's love and grace we feel the freedom to express inexpressible groans that violence has inflicted in our souls.

The Reordering of Imagination

At the beginning of this chapter I wrote how trauma has been understood as the reconfiguration and disordering of the imagination. In the aftermath of trauma the imagination of a person is affected from that point on. In this area, the church has an important role in reordering the imagination of the person who has suffered trauma. By witnessing the places of death and life that are in the middle, reordering begins to occur. In the two occurrences I narrated above, reconciliation begins by our witnessing in compassionate presence how these two individuals were helplessly trapped in the arousal of traumatic terror and the compulsion to relive it.

The reordering of imagination is witnessing the violence and trauma in grief and compassion and then taking and reframing it in the context of Christian faith. Faith provides powerful resources to imagine a specific kind of life shaped deeply by biblical stories, rituals, and traditions.[10] As is true in the story of the serpent of bronze, people who suffered the attack of the serpents were able to help make a serpent of bronze in order to receive healing and life. Framing the stories of people today in the stories of Scripture in the context of testifier and witness can facilitate people's sense of agency and help them regain the sense of dignity and hope that was tragically taken from them.

Jones explains that framing stories of trauma in biblical stories helps us to renarrate the traumatic incidents without negating or changing what occurred. That is why rewriting the script is tremendously tricky. Jones explains that it is not forgetting the past but telling a new story out of that past where agency is returned and hope might be possible.[11]

As it happened in the case of Jorge, I was able to witness his feelings of panic and anger in a way that he felt I was right there with him in total acceptance. Little by little, as he began to tell me his story in a more specific way, he was for the first time in a context of grace with his story and identity being received by me. I was able to express the profound respect I had for him and how, even in the midst of this wilderness, the presence of God was still with him. I couldn't look at the world, at him, and at our relationship in the same way after he narrated the events that had tormented him for so long.

We are called to tell our stories to one another in the communal context of grace and compassion. As we do that, we discover that our imaginations continue being formed and reordered from the violence and trauma we have experienced into the luminosity and brightness of grace that indwells in us. Reconciliation is the journey of encountering life and death all together at the same time. We are called to witness in compassion and grace the trauma of others so that a new door can be opened in order to rewrite the ruptured stories touched by violence and injustice. And perhaps then, we might be attentive to the gentle but still powerful work of the Spirit witnessing sweet glimpses of the mystery and calling of becoming gradually reconciled with one another in Jesus Christ.

Notes

1. This is not the real name of the person; I am changing names to protect the confidentiality of people.

2. Shelley Rambo, *Spirit and Trauma: A Theology of Remaining* (Louisville: Westminster John Knox, 2010), 11.

3. Rambo, *Spirit and Trauma*, 7.

4. Serene Jones, *Trauma and Grace: Theology in a Ruptured World* (Louisville: Westminster John Knox, 2009), 12.

5. Rambo, *Spirit and Trauma*, 1.

6. Jones, *Trauma and Grace*, 20.

7. Rambo, *Spirit and Trauma*, 7.

8. Peter Rollins, *The Divine Magician: The Disappearance of Religion and the Discovery of Faith* (New York: Howard Books, 2015), 33.

9. Stanley Hauerwas, *Working with Words: On Learning to Speak Christian* (Eugene, OR: Cascade Books, 2011), 3.

10. Jones, *Trauma and Grace*, 20.

11. Jones, *Trauma and Grace*, 21.

PART 2

Strategies for
Building Intercultural
Churches and Ministries

CHAPTER 6

Beyond Resurrection Sunday

Rev. Sheila Sholes-Ross

On Resurrection Sunday of 2015, I stood in the pulpit of First Baptist Church, Pittsfield, Massachusetts, and noticed a difference. This was my second Easter Sunday as the thirtieth pastor of the church. I am the first female and first African American pastor of this predominantly white church. How was the 2015 Easter Sunday different? The congregation was more diverse than on Easter Sunday of 2014. On that 2015 Resurrection Sunday the congregation included people who were white, African American, African, Hispanic, Asian American, Italian American, and Asian. There was generational diversity, too, with babies and Baby Boomers; members of the Silent Generation (1925–1945) and those of the New Silent Generation (2000/2001–present, also called Generation Z); young adults from the Millennial generation (1980–2000) and from Generation X (1965–1979); and even a smattering of folks from the G.I. Generation (born 1900–1924).[1]

The progressive New England church in which I serve is located in a city with a 2015/16 population of 44,737 people. Of this population, 39,516 are white (88 percent). There are 2,369 black or African American people (5 percent). The 2,225 Latinas/os make up 4 percent of the population. The Asian population at 550 people is 1 percent of the total. The Pittsfield 2016 demographics specify that other races make up the remaining population.[2] Therefore, any aspect of true diversity in this church should include the racial and ethnic breakdown of the city at large.

The 2015 Resurrection Sunday at First Baptist Church of Pittsfield was filled with excitement over the multiracial, multicultural, and intergenerational diversity of the congregation. After the worship service one public official in attendance stated, "I have visited many churches in and out of this area, and I have never seen anything like this before in worship. This is wonderful!"

Then the Sundays after Resurrection Sunday arrived.

Exhilaration turned into ongoing letdowns during the Sundays following that exciting Resurrection Sunday worship service. The church's greeters and ushers asked, "Where are all of those wonderful people we had on Easter Sunday? And where are the young people who brought such life to the morning? Where are they?"

As a part of my response to them, I decided to reflect upon what may have occurred and how to implement a more formal means to create continued inclusiveness of diverse people at First Baptist Church. And because I have a deep interest in developing strategies and sharing any findings with other churches struggling with the same issues, I hope to contribute to the creation of a mechanism for improving inclusivity in churches. New strategies and worship approaches can bring about a change that encourages people who only marginally attend worship services to attend more regularly. We can develop these strategies to promote an acceptance of greater racial and ethnic inclusivity in communities. As culturally different people, we can move from monocultural styles of worship that hinder inclusivity to intercultural styles that attract a diversity of people.

Can we change our learned and accepted behavior? I believe we can and will change if we follow Jesus' example. Jesus interacted with everyone who was willing to interact with him. Jesus blessed the faith of a Roman soldier (Matthew 5:8-13) and of a Syrophoenician woman (Mark 7:24-30); he spoke with a Samaritan woman at a well and then accepted the hospitality of her town (John 4:1-42); he touched those considered to be unclean under the law—lepers and epileptics, those afflicted in mind and spirit and those with disfigured or crippled bodies; he befriended those marginalized and ostracized by society—tax collectors and sinners; he ministered to Gentiles and Samaritans. Jesus demonstrated the highest level of community. As followers of Jesus, we can work to develop intercultural worship communities.

Many of us as pastors have been called to establish multiracial and intercultural churches—all in the context of church dynamics relating to change and comfort zones. Martin Luther King Jr. often noted that 11 o'clock Sunday morning worship was the most segregated time of the week in the United States. I believe this self-induced segregation comes from fundamental issues of comfort and familiarity that, at times, connect "C and E" (Christmas and Easter) congregant participation to limited cultural diversity in church worship services. "C and E" church attendees should be factored into the implementation of intercultural churches because of their consistency in attendance during these two times of the year.

At a lecture by noted *Washington Post* journalist Eugene Robinson, I asked a question related to the implementation of church diversity. Robinson answered, "Accept there will always be issues of pressure and stress when there is an attempt to implement and effect change to a person's comfort zones and formal areas of familiarity."[3] This response speaks to accepting the difficult challenge of eliminating racial segregation on Sunday mornings. There will be pressure not to implement intercultural worship and stress in bringing together different cultures on Sunday mornings for worship.

The apostle Paul says that he became "all things to all people" (1 Corinthians 9:22), and he emphasized that in Christ, "there is no longer Jew or Greek" (Galatians 3:28). It is humanly impossible to become all things, but churches must reach beyond comfort zones and familiarity to connect to people in the context of who they are. That is how the twenty-first-century church will meet the varied needs of people from different races and cultures.

Paul's words, "there is no longer Greek or Jew," lead me to believe that strategies can be implemented in Christian churches to allow us to become one in Christ across differences. Making this oneness a reality must include ongoing discussions and transparency. Ultimately, it must include people who are willing to risk losing power and control because such discussion can lead to change. Conversations must also include those people who will consider leaving the church they have known for years if any aspect of change is even considered. All people must be encouraged to come to the table for honest and transparent discussions if real change is going to happen.

During weeks of exploration following the 2015 Easter worship service, I considered the following: (1) Identify strategies used to bring together a diverse intercultural congregation on the 2015 Resurrection Sunday, (2) Identify strategies to ensure continued intercultural worship, (3) Review issues associated with traditional mindsets and non-acceptance of cultural diversity, (4) Acknowledge that moving to intercultural worship must be intentional, and (5) Explore the need for resources and support to clergy in developing intercultural churches.

Strategies for the 2015 Resurrection Sunday

Resurrection Sunday at First Baptist Church of Pittsfield may have been outside the norm, but what I have observed is that many people choose their comfort zones for worship, especially for high holiday services such as Easter. The white people who chose to come to First Baptist on that day came because of their connection to the church or were invited by another white person. I believe the African Americans chose to attend on that Easter Sunday because of me, an African American woman, who invited them. In my everyday circles, I invited African Americans and other people of color to the 2015 Resurrection Sunday worship service. I provided business cards to people in grocery stores and every community venue in which I was a participant. The congregation was diverse that morning also because current members invited family members, friends, and C and E Christians of varied cultures. Generational diversity came from family members' desire to be together on this special occasion. Personal invitations were essential.

Marketing and community involvement were also crucial strategies for implementing intercultural worship on that Resurrection Sunday of 2015. During the 2015 Lenten season, the local newspaper published an article focusing on my call to become the pastor of a multiracial and intercultural church. This article brought significant attention to the church. Many people of color stated they became interested in coming to the church when they read the article. My community work, along with my being the first female and African American pastor of the church, influenced the paper to publish this article. For example, Rabbi Joshua Breindel and I have joined together to work across religions in addressing racism and other -isms in Pittsfield.

Also during the 2015 First Baptist Church Resurrection Sunday worship service, we included black contemporary music along with traditional Eurocentric anthems, and I celebrated (an enthusiastic style of preaching) a little more during my sermon because of an increased attendance of people of color in the congregation. I used a more celebratory style of preaching (in the black community this is known as "it"), and I was excited about providing "it." From the response of the diverse people attending the worship service, the music and the sermon met the needs of the people.

The church's history of diversity also contributed to the intercultural worship service on Resurrection Sunday of 2015. *The History of the First Baptist Church of Pittsfield* documents that the church has long had people of color as members.[4] A current African American member of the church, who has attended the church ever since she was a child, remains a member with her family. This member, whose long service is documented in the church's history, told me she was intentional in inviting family and friends to the 2015 Resurrection Sunday worship service.

Although the church has had racial diversity for many years, when I became pastor in 2014, the congregational membership was mainly composed of white middle-class people known for their welcoming and affirming posture toward lesbian, gay, bisexual, transgender, and queer people (LGBTQ). The church, affiliated with the Alliance of Baptists (AOB) and American Baptist Churches of the United States of America (ABCUSA), is a progressive congregation with its acceptance of the LGBTQ community and acceptance of women in ministry. This attitude of accepting diversity laid the groundwork for intercultural worship.

Strategies for Continued Intercultural Worship

A strategy essential to the development of intercultural churches is representation of diverse cultures in leadership and worship styles. Churches cannot expect to attract people of varied races and cultures if their leaders and worship styles reflect only one culture. For example, welcoming celebratory styles of African American worship, along with styles of other cultures, and including people of various cultures in leadership will contribute to intercultural communities.

In the process of becoming intercultural, churches can adopt a strategy of connecting with other churches of differing worship styles. Exposure to different worship environments broadens understanding and appreciation of various worship styles. Ministers and congregations can build relationships in order to conduct a worship exchange: visiting the other's church with the sharing of pulpits and music.

Outreach ministries also contribute to building a multiracial and intercultural congregation. Services to meet changing societal needs benefit the congregation and the community at large. For example, Black Lives Matter ministries, along with ministries to address poverty, mental health, and other community needs are all critical for the twenty-first-century church desiring to reach a diversity of cultures.

Focus groups that include people of diverse cultures can support the development of intercultural churches. Such groups will stimulate intercultural conversation and provide information that can increase participation of people from diverse cultures. These groups can offer valuable insight into people's viewpoints relating to intercultural worship. Focus groups will allow people to express needs and concerns regarding worship changes. For all focus groups, a facilitator who is not a church leader will be beneficial to ensure a non-biased and objective process. The focus group participants can become encouraged to inspire family members, friends, and associates to help create an intercultural church. Also, focus groups can benefit a church if they are encouraged to seek information from their communities regarding lack of interest in church participation and obstacles to intercultural ministry. Properly facilitated, transparent focus group discussions will provide vital information for implementing effectual intercultural worship.

Along with focus groups to promote non-judgmental conversations, clergy can initiate conversations with individual congregants, especially with those members who are uncomfortable in group settings. Honest conversations will provide insight into changes needed to implement intercultural worship.

Marketing is another vital strategy for the implementation of multiracial and intercultural churches, including intergenerational marketing. Marketing to increase a church's diversity cannot be the sole responsibility of the pastor, even if the pastor is a member of a specific minority. All kinds of media, including websites and social media such as Facebook, need to be included in marketing strategies. Other valuable marketing tools include press releases and religious community newspaper boards, along with personal invitations to friends and family and all people with whom one comes into contact. A promotional talk sheet describing church ministries and special programs can help people with these personal invitations. Visual images in all online and print media must illustrate the church's racial, gender, and generational diversity. Marketing must be targeted to all cultures, genders, and generations.

Hindrances to Intercultural Ministry

"Please do not ask me to move beyond my comfort zone. You do know that change is difficult, and I just do not like change! Let me keep my same old church—when I do attend." A traditional mindset like this may not be expressed, but it is apparent when I look out from the pulpit and see familiar faces sitting in their same spots Sunday after Sunday.

Traditional worship mindsets are often difficult to uncover. Such mindsets of non-regular church attendees during high holiday periods may include: "Okay, I'm going to church since it is the Christmas or Easter holiday, but I will attend the church in which I feel the most comfortable, and where I'm like others in worship." Of course, this learned comfort zone is usually not stated. Regular church attendees often feel awkward about inviting people to their worship services; crossing color and culture lines can increase such discomfort. Some congregants have told me, "I'm uncomfortable with inviting people to church."

In order to change traditional mindsets, we should remember that Jesus was a rabble-rouser who challenged conventional comfort zones, especially among those who were accustomed to setting the rules—the rich, the powerful, the religious elite. The Gospel of Luke records Jesus speaking of being anointed to preach good news to the poor and to proclaim freedom for the prisoners (Luke 4:18). Many church members are out of their comfort zones when called to interact with people of different cultures, but Jesus points the way. As followers of Jesus, we can also change the norm in order to develop, implement, and sustain intercultural churches.

To create intercultural ministries we may need to move beyond our comfort zones in our social relationships. I inquire in church and other social settings, "How many people of other races and ethnicities do you socialize with?" I am often surprised by the responses. For example, many white people respond that they socialize with two or fewer people of other races. And with people of color, the responses are similar. If there is cross-cultural socialization, it usually comes from interracial marriages and partnerships, school, and sports events.

Declining church membership and the resulting decline in financial support often result in reduced church staff. It's difficult for one full-time pastor and a handful of volunteer leaders to conduct all the work necessary to develop intercultural congregations. Implementing proposed strategies for attracting people of diverse races and cultures may prove challenging. Traditional mindsets may take a long time to change, and a limited church staff and volunteers make the process even slower.

We can, however, begin by encouraging people to move beyond their comfort zones and past traditionalism to create diverse communities. Such communities unite people across cultures and provide a powerful model beyond the four walls of churches.

Intentionality: A Necessity for Intercultural Worship

Creating intercultural worship necessitates intentional planning to include various cultures and worship styles in Sunday services. Everyone from the church's music director to leaders of ministries and committees must take part in the process of developing worship services inclusive of diverse races and cultures. If only one culture is included in the worship style and leadership, then other cultures will feel dishonored and stop participating in the church.

Born and raised in New Orleans, Louisiana, I grew up with access to diverse worship services. I experienced "spirit-filled" worship in a local Catholic church in the early 1980s. Yes, a Catholic church—one that was historically black. One of my friends was a member there, and often I was her invited guest. I was in awe of the music and always moved by the priest's homily. A different domination, but similar cultures, provided for a different learning experience.

A brief review of the Christian church and slavery will help place this experience in context. Many of the black slaves attended white-dominated churches, but outside of the church institution, in their own lives and spaces, they also "practiced a covert and distinctive form of worship—characterized by enthusiastic preaching, spirituals, and a call-and response format reminiscent of West African practice. This was often viewed as an 'invisible institution,' because of its style."[5] Many of the black churches today, across denominations, still practice such enthusiastic styles of worship.

Noted preacher and reconciliation advocate Tony Evans also places such worship styles into perspective: "When African Americans consider the care and protection God supplies, especially in light of their socioeconomic plight and history, it is difficult not to be expressive."[6] Such expression may take various forms, including clapping, shouting, dancing, testifying, and the classic call-and-response interaction between members of the congregation and the preacher. "Well! Amen! Hallelujah! Tell It! Say that! Take your time!" are just a few familiar congregational responses that affirm or encourage the Word of God from the preacher.

Evans goes on to speculate that many Anglos lack understanding regarding call and response in connection with celebratory deliverance of a message by a black preacher.[7] As a black preacher, I find it difficult to hear from white people that this type of worship is not meditative. A belief that only silence during worship reflects an appropriate spirit or response in worship denies cultural differences. While they are right that silence is one aspect of worship, I agree with Evans that outspoken celebration found in black churches is due to African Americans' gratefulness for deliverances from slavery and other forms of oppression.

Clergy must encourage, and lead, congregants to explore and understand cultural differences and similarities in worship styles. With such intentionality, together they can develop an intercultural appreciation. Then congregations can move forward to include a variety of cultural expressions in their worship services.

Support for Clergy Developing Intercultural Churches

Pastors who take the risks of intercultural ministry need resources and support. This support may especially be needed if the pastor is part of a minority culture in the church. Support can help leaders remain faithful to their calling as God moves the church toward becoming intercultural.

Clergy and other church leaders may benefit from conferences and workshops that address intercultural challenges and that explore strategies for evolving toward intentional intercultural ministry. Existing intercultural congregations can offer mentorships and provide resources to developing congregations. There is a need for intercultural networks to encourage development of intercultural churches.

One group, Equity for Women in the Church Community, a newly formed 501(c)(3), aspires to provide support for intercultural church development. The mission of this ecumenical and culturally diverse organization is to facilitate equal representation of clergywomen as pastors of intercultural churches in order to transform church and society. Equity for Women in the Church is intentionally intercultural with diverse races and cultures represented in the leadership and in all aspects of the organization. One project of this organization is to provide financial support to clergywomen who create new and renewed intercultural churches. Equity for Women in the Church also partners with seminaries and theological schools to provide resources for developing intercultural ministries.

Strong personal support systems are critical for clergy focusing on intercultural work. For example, I have support systems such as a wonderful and encouraging husband, a biological sister and brother, and surrogate sisters and brothers across the country who understand my call to intercultural ministry. I remain in close contact with my mentor, a pastor of a historically African American church, to receive comfort and encouragement and to bounce ideas around. However, I still have a vital need to connect with clergypersons who have succeeded in the reversal of segregated Sunday morning worship services.

Although I feel called by God to pastor an intercultural congregation, I value support as I work with my current congregation, which is predominantly white, to become more culturally diverse. I have been an associate minister in a predominantly African American congregation, with approximately 1 percent white and other races. Even though this congregation included diverse styles of worship, the dominant culture dictated the predominant worship style. Congregations need resources and models as they move beyond familiarity and comfort toward understanding, acceptance, inclusion, and celebration of cultural differences in Christian churches.

Summary

Intercultural ministry entails exploring strategies for bringing together varied cultures, giving equal power to each, and meeting diverse people's needs. Strategies include worship leaders and styles that represent varied races and cultures, marketing through all forms of media and personal invitations, outreach ministries to meet needs of diverse people, and focus groups to provide opportunities for transparent conversations regarding worship changes.

It may be difficult to introduce varied worship styles if the church has been accustomed mainly to the style of one culture. Clergy and church members can challenge one another to move beyond their comfort zones and traditional mindsets that hinder intercultural ministry. Jesus, the rabble-rouser, provides a model for liberating people from stifling conventions and for interacting with people of diverse cultures.

Intentionality is vital to the development of intercultural churches. Clergy and congregants must be intentional in exploring cultural differences in order to develop appreciation of various worship styles. Then they can move forward to include diverse cultures in worship services and in all areas of the church.

Resources and support are necessary for the development of intercultural churches. Support may include conferences and workshops, partnerships with intercultural congregations, financial resources from organizations and institutions, and personal relationships.

With the hard work of people inspired by love of God and humanity to embrace liberating change, intercultural churches will develop and flourish. Such churches will not be an exception to the rule but will lead the way for changing Sunday morning from the most segregated time of the week to the most inclusive. Beyond Resurrection Sunday, we will find thriving intercultural churches.

Notes

1. Matt Rosenberg, "Names of Generations," accessed October 24, 2016, http://geography.about.com/od/populationgeography/qt/generations.htm.

2. Accessed October 24, 2016, https://suburbanstats.org/population/massachusetts /how-many-people-live-in-pittsfield.

3. Sheila Sholes-Ross, question to Eugene Robinson, Temple Anshe Amunim Lecture Series, August, Pittsfield, Massachusetts, 2014.

4. Doris Nutt, *The History of the First Baptist Church of Pittsfield* (Pittsfield, MA: Memorial Historical Committee of First Baptist Church, 1982), 2.

5. Bret E. Carroll, *The Routledge Historical Atlas of Religion in America*, Routledge Atlases of American History, Mark C. Carnes, series editor (New York, Routledge, 2000), 85–86.

6. Tony Evans, *Oneness Embraced: Through the Eyes of Tony Evans: A Fresh Look at Reconciliation, the Kingdom, and Justice* (Chicago: Moody Publishers, 2011), 177.

7. Evans, *Oneness Embraced*, 177.

CHAPTER 7

An Experiment in Radical Religious Openness

Rev. Dr. Brad R. Braxton

On October 8, 2011, fifty-five people gathered in a Baltimore library to initiate an experiment in radical religious openness. A library, a repository of ancient wisdom and emerging knowledge, seemed a perfect place to ask a poignant question: Is it possible for a community to love and serve God apart from the cultural discord and theological dogma that can make religion so dangerous? We dreamed a big dream about a bold, new congregation whose chief characteristic would be openness—openness to radically inclusive love, courageous social justice activism, and compassionate inter-faith collaboration. At the meeting's conclusion, The Open Church of Maryland had begun.

Five years later, The Open Church is a viable faith community. With purpose and passion, The Open Church is pushing cultural boundaries and challenging theological assumptions. For example, The Open Church 1) considers the weekly worship service as a "political assembly" for creating citizens who are preparing to live in God's inbreaking *kin*-dom;[1] 2) supports the moral and civic equality of LGBTQ persons; 3) sensitizes congregants about social injustices such as classism; and 4) embraces interfaith collaboration as an antidote to Christian arrogance and imperialism.

At a typical gathering of The Open Church, a thirty-something, white, lesbian agnostic with a master's degree might sit next to a blue-collar heterosexual black nationalist in his sixties as they collaborate to bring healing and hope to Baltimore's blighted communities. The Open Church is increasingly becoming a resource for local and national initiatives concerning diversity and inclusion. For example, The Open Church's advocacy for marriage equality received national attention through a PBS interview.

On the one hand, our progress in building an intercultural church has been remarkable. On the other hand, as the founding senior pastor, I realize how precarious the experiment still is. Some congregants remain reticent about the joyful embrace of radical inclusion and the discarding of problematic religious perspectives. For example, although there is a healthy balance between heterosexual and LGBTQ persons in the congregation, some congregants worry that The Open Church is (or will become) the "gay church." Additionally, the emphasis on Jesus' humanity and questioning of Jesus' divinity, dismissal of narrow definitions of biblical authority, and use of gender-inclusive language (especially when referencing God) have sparked discomfort and respectful resistance in some persons. And, some persons who say they desire an intercultural experience renege when they understand how many dimensions of culture and diversity The Open Church is audaciously exploring.

At The Open Church (and for the purposes of this chapter), culture is understood in an expansive way that includes and extends considerably beyond race/ethnicity. Sheila Davaney defines culture as "the process by which meaning is produced, contended for, and continually renegotiated and the context in which individual and communal identities are mediated and brought into being."[2] The Open Church is predominantly African American, with a growing presence of white members. Nevertheless, The Open Church is intercultural because of the conscious embrace of diverse cultural factors that mediate meaning and delineate identities.

This chapter will explore the historical background, theological commitments, and religious practices that have bolstered The

Open Church's development, guided by our vision statement recited in worship.

The Open Church Vision Statement

All: The Open Church is a sacred place where those who are hurting, confused, and in need can find healing and hope, regardless of color, culture, or creed.

Leader: It is a wide place where "Abraham's family"—Christians, Jews, and Muslims—can dialogue with Buddhists and Bahá'is and where Hindus can dialogue with Humanists.

All: The Open Church is a joyful place where children, seniors, migrant workers, people experiencing homelessness, and scholars eagerly learn from and teach one another.

Leader: It is a safe place where varied ethnicities and capabilities, genders and sexual identities, social and economic groups gather in peace to break bread at Christ's Communion Table, as we break down stereotypes.

All: As sacred siblings born to our Heavenly Father who is Divine Mother of us all, we practice radically inclusive love that proclaims and builds up the "_kin_-dom of God."

(Auto)Biography Is Theology

During the last fifty years, contextual theologies (e.g., black theology, women's theologies [feminist/womanist/mujerista], postmodern theology, postcolonial theology, queer theology) have insisted that responsible theological discourse must be grounded in our personal stories and cultural histories and context.[3] My context is a priceless text to be thoroughly excavated for its insights and impact. The stories of who we are influence the stories of who we understand God to be. (Auto)biography is theology.

The Two Churches That Led to the Third

The Open Church is the third congregation that I have shepherded. The Open Church would not exist were it not for important experiences in my previous two churches: Douglas Memorial Community Church and The Riverside Church.

Douglas Memorial Community Church (1995–2000). My first pastorate was at the Douglas Memorial Community Church, a medium-sized, nondenominational church in downtown Baltimore. At Douglas Church, I inherited a congregation of tough-minded, tenderhearted believers who were ready to embrace change and welcome me as their spiritual leader. Many beautiful things blossomed across five years. For example, two hundred people joined the congregation. An intellectually robust Wednesday Bible study was created with a regular attendance in excess of one hundred persons. In addition, we engaged exciting interfaith initiatives with Baltimore's Jewish community.

Through a sacred partnership between people and pastor, Douglas Church had been revitalized.[4] I came to Douglas Church as a scholar. In 2000, I left as a scholar and a pastor. It was now time for me to mentor other scholars and pastors.

Having completed my PhD at Emory University in 1999, I was called in 2000 to the ministry of university teaching and served on two distinguished divinity school faculties—four years as an assistant professor at Wake Forest University and four years as an associate professor at Vanderbilt University. In those years, I taught preaching and biblical studies to brilliant students; published three books; made three pilgrimages to Africa; and clarified the intellectual and spiritual dimensions of my progressive, intercultural agenda.

I thoroughly enjoyed my professorial ministry. Yet, I knew that at some point the professor had to return to the pastorate. The call to what I thought would be my second and final pastorate came in the fall of 2008.

The Riverside Church (2008–2009). I was called in 2008 to be the sixth senior minister of The Riverside Church in New York City. The Riverside Church is a large, historic, intercultural institution. At the age of thirty-nine, I was the youngest senior minister ever called by the congregation and the second African American. In spite of the challenges of my nine-month tenure at Riverside, I count it a privilege to have served that remarkable congregation.

After several months of serving as senior minister, long-standing internal tensions severely hindered progress in executing the church's stated intercultural mission and vision. Undoubtedly, I made tactical leadership errors. Nevertheless, the assaults on my professional pedigree and leadership, orchestrated by a small, organized, and influential group of congregants, revealed that I was a lightning rod for internal congregational storms that had raged for decades. Rather than create additional strife, I voluntarily resigned from the pastorate of The Riverside Church in the hope that all parties would benefit from new beginnings. My rapid resignation resulted in shock and sadness among many congregants.

Seven years have passed since my departure from Riverside. For approximately five of those seven years, Riverside was without a permanent senior minister. Amy Butler, my pastoral successor, is the first woman to serve as Riverside's senior minister. She has made generous gestures to foster reconciliation between that congregation and me, including my participation in her pastoral installation in 2014 and Riverside's eighty-fifth anniversary in 2015. Since my departure, hindsight has taken on its 20/20 character. I have increasing clarity concerning how the experience at Riverside prepared me for The Open Church.

During my yearlong candidacy for Riverside's pastorate, I read accounts of Riverside's history and interviewed many people familiar with the congregation.[5] As part of my due diligence, I searched for clues to Riverside's institutional DNA. In addition to Riverside's splendid external reputation, my investigation revealed an internal narrative of congregational divisiveness, unclear boundaries between clergy and lay leaders, and an ineffectual governance structure. For some people in the church, the most sacred text was not the Bible but instead the congregation's bylaws.

These issues of power became acutely pronounced during the tenure of the third senior minister, Ernest Campbell. Governance matters prompted Campbell to resign from Riverside in 1976.[6] Governance issues also beset the pastorate of the fourth senior minister, William Sloane Coffin.[7]

If Ernest Campbell and William Sloane Coffin, white pastors, struggled with these governance issues when the church remained predominantly white, one can imagine how these governance issues intensified during James Forbes's tenure and my own—a time when Riverside was led by its first African American pastors. During Forbes's historic pastorate, the racial dynamics shifted significantly, and Riverside became a predominantly black congregation.[8] The shockwaves of that shift reverberated and complicated already contested governance matters by unearthing the heretofore unexpressed "white anxiety" that often occurs when intercultural ministry decenters white people and white cultural priorities.

Intercultural Lessons Learned at The Riverside Church

This abbreviated retelling of portions of my Riverside experience is germane to the founding of The Open Church in crucial ways. First, my Riverside pastorate compelled me to think more explicitly and theologically about issues of power when building an intercultural community.

The Power in Understanding Power. Congregational leaders often deem issues of power as unsavory at best or evil at worst. "Spiritual people" supposedly should not be preoccupied with power. Defining power by its worst manifestations, many congregations operate with problematic understandings of power and avoid the-ological analyses of power. This avoidance can result in power imbalances, where unhealthy amounts of power are concentrated in the hands of an individual or a small group.

Furthermore, until issues of power are addressed, congregations interested in intercultural ministry often confuse representation for diversity. The influx of a minority community into a majority com-munity does not necessarily equate to diversity. That influx might simply mean that there is greater intercultural representation in that community. Diversity genuinely surfaces when minority groups are represented in sufficient numbers to organize and thus challenge and change power structures in a community.

Even though Riverside's racial demographics had shifted, its overall cultural ethos and approach to religious practices remained firmly anchored in white cultural narratives and priori-ties. Racial justice educators and activists have long noted that covert, institutional racism—not overt, individual racism—is the more difficult form of racial injustice to overcome. Joseph Barndt insists, "The distinctive mark of racism is power—collective, sys-temic, societal power."[9]

Barndt's framework explains why even my small attempts at Riverside to question or decenter the assumed superiority of white perspectives and approaches aroused serious opposition, and the leaders of the opposition on some occasions were black people. Internalized oppression is often subtle and runs very deep. This explains why some women, ironically, are fierce opponents of fem-inist liberation efforts and why some people of color vigorously oppose efforts to dethrone white privilege.[10]

For an intercultural agenda to thrive in a congregation, leaders and congregants must consider power an appropriate topic for the-ologically nuanced discussion. Leaders must attend to issues of power with the same care that they attend to liturgical practices such as preaching and praying. I now tell persons aspiring to be pastors, especially in intercultural contexts: "Spend as much time with the bylaws as you do with the Bible. Both the 'devil' who can harm you and the 'angel' who can heal you are in the details about how power is understood and applied in a community."

A Nimble Governance Structure. My experience at Riverside also influenced my desire to create an intercultural congregation with a nimble governance structure. In the years between leaving Riverside and founding The Open Church, I mused: How can a congregation have governance structures that are responsible to fiduciary matters yet open to the leadership of the Holy Spirit?

As Jesus says to Nicodemus in John 3:8, the wind of the Spirit blows wherever it wills. The unruly Spirit often disrespects the decorum and deliberations of the parliamentary procedures pre-scribed by *Robert's Rules of Order*. Governance structures can become so burdensome that they prevent a congregation from dis-cerning the unexpected thing that God wants to do. Envisioning The Open Church and its governance structures, I regularly called to mind poignant observations from the theologian Justo González: "The function of the Spirit is not so much to create the structures and procedures by which the church must live forever, but rather to break *open* structures so that the church may be obe-dient as it faces each new challenge."[11]

When faced with the opportunity of embracing genuine inter-cultural ministry, many faith communities across the millennia have said a defiant no to these opportunities. Their negations often have been inscribed institutionally in restrictive gover-nance structures that frustrate the boundary-breaking move-ment of the Spirit.

My experience at Riverside was both humbling and hurtful. Yet, that painful episode made me eager to envision a new intercultur-al faith community characterized by permissive power structures that enabled the default answer of a congregation to be yes.

The Open Church: Pursuing Openness on Purpose

After my departure from Riverside, I relocated with my family to Chicago, where I took a year-long professional sabbatical. After the sabbatical, I served for two years as Distinguished Visiting Scholar at McCormick Theological Seminary. McCormick administrators, faculty, staff, and students were invaluable dialogue partners as The Open Church's vision was conceived and born.

I wanted to form an intercultural community held together by three core theological commitments:

■ **Progressive Ministry:** Progressive ministry believes that sacred texts and authoritative traditions must be critically engaged and continually reinterpreted in light of contemporary circumstances, or religion becomes a relic.

■ **Prophetic Ministry:** Prophetic ministry insists that God desires to save us not only from our personal sins but also from the systemic sins that oppress neighborhoods and nations.

■ **Pluralistic Ministry:** Pluralistic ministry is a liberating call to "uncertainty, to a sense of human and religious limitedness. It is an affirmation that what we think we know certainly and absolutely is, in fact, neither certain nor absolute."[12] By opening our hands and hearts, we make it possible to grasp, and be grasped by, larger truths.

Like sturdy beams supporting a floor, these three core commitments undergirded every aspect of The Open Church's founding meeting in October 2011. Thus, in the very foundation of the congregation is an explicit commitment to radical openness.

In the founding meeting, and subsequent meetings across these five years, we envisioned and have striven to be The Open Church, not just the The Open Door Church. Many churches have referred to themselves as "open door" churches. I do not disparage congregations with open doors. However, The Open Church has loftier ambitions in its pursuit of openness. In some churches, the doors may be open, but the windows are nailed shut through denominational dogma, burdensome bureaucracy, and an obsession with outdated orthodoxies (to name a few nails). Consequently, the free-flowing Wind cannot circulate properly, and the air becomes stagnant.

We purposed to create a church whose entire existence was open. We envisioned: A church open to any persons and perspectives that are truthful, just, and compassionate. A church open to theistic and nontheistic religions and to humanist and atheistic moral philosophies. A church open to sexual diversity so that LGBTQ persons could emerge from the closets they often inhabit in religious spaces for fear of "assault and battery" by the Bible. A church open to the courageous reimagining and embracing of the feminine dimensions of God as an act of resistance to sexism. A church open to class diversity that would enable white-collar salary workers and blue-collar shift workers to learn with and from one another.

Although openness is an obvious commitment at The Open Church, an equally central commitment buttressing our intercultural work is purpose. Purpose must be the partner to openness. In a world where so many people are closed off from opportunities, from sources of abundance, and even from one another, intercultural communities will not occur by accident. Benjamin Mays, the sage who mentored Martin Luther King Jr., understood well the irreverent insistence needed to ignite personal and social transformation across cultural boundaries. Mays remarked, "I would rather go to hell by choice than to stumble into heaven following the crowd."[13]

Too many faith communities are stumbling in their efforts to promote inclusion because they are comfortably following the crowd. They are afraid to engage in audacious, purposeful actions to create the conditions for diversity to thrive. I frequently offer in my sermons and pastoral exhortations at The Open Church my contemporary remix of Mays's insight on purpose:

If radical inclusion sends me to hell, then I am going to hell *on purpose*, and I will take the express train there! God, if your heaven is exclusive, then it is a place I would rather not be because *all* my sacred siblings are not welcome there.

This brazen statement encapsulates the ultimate sacredness of openness for me. In my theology, an inclusive hell is more sacred than an exclusive heaven. Below, I chronicle briefly examples of how The Open Church is purposefully supporting diversity and inclusion.

Wrestling with Biblical Authority on Purpose

At The Open Church, we question the Bible and acknowledge its moral ambiguities. We often say, "Not everything in the 'Good Book' is good news." We intentionally renounce the regrettable role that the Bible has played in legitimizing vilification and violence, especially as it relates to women and LGBTQ people.

We are constructing notions of biblical authority that invite people to engage the Bible with intellectual honesty as well as reverence. In an early sermon at The Open Church, I placed biblical authority front and center in the congregation's ministry of inclusion:

> In my estimation, biblical authority is about engagement with the Book, not necessarily agreement with the Book. . . . Because I know what I believe and in whom I believe, I can listen to you talk about what you believe and in whom you believe. Biblical authority simply means, "Let's engage!". . .
>
> So, as we ponder the meanings of biblical authority, I will not coerce you to agree with me. Rather I offer my perspectives as a catalyst for you to voice your perspectives, with the hope that from multiple perspectives, we might assemble some fragments of truth.[14]

Creating a Culture of Inquiry on Purpose

The Open Church also fosters an atmosphere where we lovingly question one another. Creating a culture of healthy, respectful inquiry is a critical component of the intercultural experience. We conceive of The Open Church as a republic—a sacred, political assembly where we are learning to share power for the sake of a better world. A key congregational mantra is: "At The Open Church, *everyone* is a minister." Accordingly, everyone's voice is crucial as we discern collaboratively what the good news is and how the good news compels us to act.

We amplify the voices of everyone by frequently holding dialogue-driven services dealing with major theological and social issues such as the humanity/divinity of Jesus, the interplay of sexuality and spirituality, immigration, homelessness, and violence. We regularly place in the bulletin discussion questions based on the worship service and sermon for that day, and the question-and-answer period occurs immediately after the sermon. On some occasions, discussion questions and the dialogue around them constitute the entire worship service.

At The Open Church, the invitation to dialogue is as important as the invitation to discipleship. Kathleen Neal Cleaver, the freedom fighter and legal scholar, said, "No one can speak truth to power until they know what is true."[15] In order to know what is true, we must listen to, reason with, and question one another.

Dethroning Sexist Language on Purpose

Language possesses both life-giving and death-dealing power. Thus, what we say and how we say it are matters of great moral consequence. At The Open Church, we embrace gender-inclusive language as a moral act that creates an inclusive environment. Early in the development of our congregation, I wrote the following statement and placed it in the bulletin:

As Christians, we are a people of the word. According to Genesis 1, God created in the beginning with the spoken word. We gather in worship to listen to and wrestle with the words of scripture in the hope that those words will lead us to the living word of God's truth for us here and now.

The lyrics of many of our sacred songs were composed at a time when God was thought to be "male." Unfortunately, the exclusive imaging of God as male has contributed to the horrific injustice of sexism, the assumed superiority of males. This injustice affects us all, but it especially injures women and girls.

Yet, we know that God is neither male nor female. God is a living Spirit. So, at The Open Church, we value inclusive language as a reminder that none of our terms for God can accurately capture God's majestic presence and infinite essence. There is nothing wrong with calling God "Father," but in fairness we shouldn't mind calling God "Mother" either. God is a good God. Yes, *She* is! Furthermore, when we have the opportunity to avoid pronouns, we should not mind simply referring to God as God.

Eboo Patel, a friend and noted interfaith educator, intimates that our language practices and stories can either build bombs to destroy or bridges to unite.[16]

Opening the Communion Table on Purpose

At The Open Church, the table where we share Holy Communion is radically open. In some Christian traditions, there are strict preconditions for who can serve and partake of this simple meal of bread and wine (or juice) that symbolizes the price that Jesus paid to justly resist injustice. For example, in some Christian denominations only ordained clergy and authorized lay leaders are permitted to consecrate and serve the meal. Additionally, only baptized believers can partake of the communion elements.

At The Open Church anyone can serve Holy Communion, and everyone who desires the meal is welcome at the table. In a world full of hungry and thirsty people, it is unconscionable to me to serve a meal, even a symbolic one, and not attempt to invite as many willing people to the table as possible. Furthermore, in light of Jesus' deep affection for children (e.g., Matthew 19:13-15), placing children's hands on Holy Communion makes the meal even holier. Thus, at The Open Church, we especially delight in inviting children to serve the meal. I typically use some variation of the statement below to invite the community to the table:

> At this table, no reservations are needed, and no priority seating is allowed. At The Open Church, God's welcome table is open, radically open, to whosoever will. You don't even have to believe in God to come to this table, because even if you don't believe in God, God still believes in you. Come!

The response to our radically open table has been overwhelmingly positive, even if some congregants come to the table questioning why they previously belonged to faith communities that placed fences around a table designed to foster communion.

Next Steps: Playing A *Love Supreme* on Purpose

I am thankful for how far The Open Church has come and mindful of the long journey ahead. As the congregation's chief visionary, my primary responsibility is romantic in nature. Pushing the boundaries toward radical religious openness will involve wooing people to open their hearts even more to a love supreme. The Open Church's vision is bold, global, and even cosmic. We believe that radically inclusive love is the heartbeat of God and the ultimate impulse in an infinite and expanding universe. Through the ages, apostles and prophets have tried to seduce us with this love.

In 1965, the acoustical apostle John Coltrane released his monumental album entitled *A Love Supreme*. With his saxophone, Coltrane preached a sermon. A love supreme—a soaring, unconditional love not detained by dogma or constrained by color or creed—is the missing note in the jam session for restorative justice and intercultural inclusion. The Open Church is a tool through which God can push boundaries. The Open Church is an instrument on which God can play *A Love Supreme* . . . on purpose!

Notes

1. Kin-dom is a term coined by feminist theologians to disrupt the unjust assumption that God is male. The term also accentuates relationality: our relationships with God and our relationships with one another. We are all *kin*folk.

2. Sheila Greeve Davaney, "Theology and the Turn to Cultural Analysis," in *Converging on Culture: Theologians in Dialogue with Cultural Analysis and Criticism*, ed. Delwin Brown, Sheila Greeve Davaney, and Kathryn Tanner (New York: Oxford University Press, 2001), 5.

3. For concise explanations of these and other contextual theologies, consult Daniel Patte, ed., *The Cambridge Dictionary of Christianity* (Cambridge: Cambridge University Press, 2010).

4. *The Baltimore Sun* chronicled Douglas Church's revitalization: David L. Greene, "Here to Have Church," *The Baltimore Sun*, July 10, 2000, accessed January 31, 2016, http://articles.baltimoresun.com/2000-07-10/news/0007100 109_1_braxton-church-pastor.

5. For example, Peter Paris et al., eds., *The History of The Riverside Church in the City of New York* (New York: New York University Press, 2004).

6. Paris et al., *History of The Riverside Church*, 46.

7. Paris et al., *History of The Riverside Church*, 47.

8. I use here the more inclusive term "black" instead of "African American" to include the appreciable number of Riverside members who are from Africa and the African diaspora.

9. Joseph Barndt, *Understanding and Dismantling Racism: The Twenty-First Century Challenge to White America* (Minneapolis: Fortress, 2007), 143–44.

10. Kwok Pui-lan, *Postcolonial Imagination and Feminist Theology* (Louisville, KY: Westminster John Knox, 2005), 43.

11. Justo L. González, "Reading from my Bicultural Place: Acts 6:1-7," in *Reading from This Place: Social Location and Biblical Interpretation in the United States*, ed. Fernando F. Segovia and Mary Ann Tolbert (Minneapolis: Fortress, 1995), 146 (emphasis added).

12. Joseph M. Webb, *Preaching and the Challenge of Pluralism* (St. Louis, MO: Chalice Press, 1998), 108.

13. Benjamin E. Mays, quoted in *Walking Integrity: Benjamin Elijah Mays, Mentor to Martin Luther King Jr.*, ed. Lawrence Edward Carter Sr. (Macon, GA: Mercer University Press, 1998), 12.

14. Brad R. Braxton, "Interpretation for Liberation: Working with the Book," preached on August 5, 2012.

15. Kathleen Neal Cleaver, quoted in *Disrupting White Supremacy from Within: White People on What We Need to Do*, ed. Jennifer Harvey, Karin A. Case, and Robin Hawley Gorsline (Cleveland: Pilgrim Press, 2004), 9.

16. Eboo Patel, *Acts of Faith: The Story of an American Muslim, the Struggle for the Soul of a Generation* (Boston: Beacon Press, 2007), xi–xix.

CHAPTER 8

Laying a Foundation for a True and Viable Intercultural Church

Rev. Christine A. Smith

When we hear the term "intercultural church," depending upon our perspective, varying images may emerge. For those in the dominant culture, seeing a few folks of different hues on Sunday morning may appear intercultural. For those in the minority, their perspective will depend upon where they are in the assimilation process. If they are comfortable and accustomed to being one of few, they too may view their church as intercultural. However, those minority individuals who desire to bring true diversity to the mix frequently find themselves bumping up against dominant culture privilege, assumptions, and hostilities.

Several factors influence whether or not a true intercultural church will or will not emerge as viable, living, thriving. The descriptors "true" and "viable" are critical to the discussion. Many churches that are simply integrated (less than 5 percent of the congregation is of another ethnicity) name themselves "multicultural." Similarly, many churches that have a variety of ethnicities on the church roll have cosmetic diversity—with varying ethnicities participating but little or no cultural representation in the worship, structure, or governance of the total congregation.

Laying a foundation for an intercultural church takes much prayer, dialogue, openness, and intentionality. In this chapter, I will share my personal pastoral experiences related to the illusion of interculturalism as well as offer practical strategies for ways churches can truly become intercultural and diverse.

Although churches in the twenty-first century appear to be increasing in diversity, many still wrestle with being intercultural. Two persistent, remaining issues are those of power and perception. If the cultures strive to be open, to dialogue, and to share interests, styles, and concerns, newcomers will experience a genuine willingness on the part of original members to work together with them and grow. Conversely, if the dominant culture perceives that an increase of minorities will mean a shift in power, they may either close ranks or flee.

My attempt to build an intercultural congregation was derailed by some of those same complications. In 2006, I was called to become the solo pastor of a small, dying, fragmented, and predominantly Euro-American Baptist congregation. I was their first female and African American pastor.

A Rough Start

As we began our journey together, cultural differences and perceptions of the role of the pastor emerged. Minorities tend to view the pastor as "called," the "shepherd, visionary, and leader of the congregation." Many Euro-American churches tend to view pastors as hired to work as directed by boards and in collaboration with the church president or moderator. We struggled with this difference of perspective.

As an African American female, I came with the awareness that being the first of anything can be challenging. The congregation was older and dying, and therefore I knew that church growth was critical. Working with the congregation to help identify areas of commonality and goals would be of utmost importance. The mountain we were climbing, however, was much steeper than I could have ever imagined. The neighborhood, although transitioning very slowly, was still predominantly Euro-American, Italian, and Catholic. People in the area resisted our attempts to invite them to worship and other programs. The fact that I was a woman and an African American greatly affected the community's perception of our church.

Another issue also muddied our proverbial waters. Although Euro-American churches are more willing than many African American congregations to hire/call an African American female pastor, they often struggle to embrace the culture she embodies. I was accustomed to a call-and-response atmosphere (verbal acknowledgements such as, "Amen!" "Yes, Lord!" "Praise God!") as I preached. Because I had served previously as a part-time worship leader/preacher for one year in another Euro-American congregation, I was somewhat prepared for the quiet, still atmosphere into which I would be immersed as pastor—but not completely.

I was not prepared for the impact preaching in what felt like an emotionally and spiritually cold atmosphere would have upon me. In fairness, my style and tone of preaching had to be an adjustment for them as well. Together, however, we pressed on.

The Challenges of New Growth

The immediate area in which the church was situated was unreceptive to the new ministry that was unfolding. The surrounding areas, however, appeared to become excited. Because of my relationships with other churches and in the community, people did begin to come and join. But the people were not Euro-American.

Initially, joy and excitement filled the air on Sunday mornings. Within six months, our congregation began to grow. Families with young adults and children began to join. Ministries were revived and developed. After about one year, we went from a congregational size of approximately forty-five to one hundred. It seemed that we were on our way, and then fears began to emerge.

The new members were predominantly African American. Although we maintained the same music (we only added a contemporary gospel ensemble that sang once a month), the same church officers, and the same order of worship, several members began to express concerns. Here are some comments to church deacons and to me: "The church is becoming too black." "If one more person shouts 'Hallelujah!' I'm leaving this church!" "When it was only a few black families here, I never thought about how *they* felt, but now that there seems to be more 'blacks' and less of 'us,' I know how they must have felt." On a Sunday morning while I stood in the back of the church in the receiving line, members still moving about in the sanctuary, one white member shouted, "*Where are all the white people?* Why aren't white people joining this church?"

I must admit, I was unprepared for the earthquakes and upheavals that erupted. I had no answers for the turmoil. I was offended, hurt, and dismayed. We prayed, cried, tried to have small-group discussions, workshops, guest speakers, and one-on-one dialogues. None of these measures worked. In fairness to the original members, the influx of new members who did not look like them must have been overwhelming. Our fragile structure was unable to bear up under the complicated labyrinth of racism and perceived power shifts. Elderly members began to die, and others (whites) began to leave. Our once-thriving ministry dwindled back down to the original number, numerically forty-five to fifty, comprised of mostly new African American members and a few of the original white members. Finances were devastated. Morale was crushed. All of this within the first two to three years of my pastorate.

Stability and Strategy

It has taken about six years for us to recover and stabilize. Recovery has been slow and challenging. It would be great to say that we began to do lots of ministry things and we lived happily ever after, but that is not the reality. We had to develop a specific, strategic prayer focus that identified clearly our current situation, what needed to happen in that season, our hopes for the future, and what was necessary to make that happen.

We prayed specifically that God would enable us to focus upon ministry and not bills. Each week we listed in the bulletin last week's offering and what we needed to cover the bills. I told the congregation, "When we get to the place where we have enough offering on Sundays to pay the bills, we will stop posting it in the bulletin." They did not like it, but it worked.

Our giving increased. Little by little, we paid off major bills. It was not enough, however, to tackle the major expenses associated with an old, drafty, deteriorating edifice. Utility bills were sky high. The roof was literally beginning to cave in. In 2013, our congregation came to the conclusion that we needed to sell the property, take the proceeds, and do a new thing. It was the best decision we could have ever made.

After a year and a half we entered into a lease/purchase agreement for our historic building with another congregation. At the conclusion of the agreement, our church will receive a lump-sum payoff that will be used to purchase a new facility. With our new income, we have been able to pay off remaining debts, pay the pastor (me) a decent salary, and begin some new ministry efforts. We are currently leasing space in a local Catholic church school building. Our prayers to focus upon ministry and not on bills have been answered.

This Far by Faith

Our congregation has become predominantly African American. We are in the process of rebuilding the ministry. Progress has been slow but steady. God has brought us through. We now understand that true interculturalism is not something that just happens but must be thought through, talked through, prayed through, and worked on. Our current evangelism and discipleship efforts are taking the above factors into prayerful consideration moving forward.

God has opened doors for intercultural ministry in our new space. The priest and parish of the Catholic church where we lease space approached us about having a joint worship service for Palm Sunday. Together we blessed the palms, shared readings from the Gospels, participated in a processional from our space to the main sanctuary, sat, sang, and prayed together in worship. While that may not sound like a big deal, it was a momentous event for two very different church cultures to come together.

When we first came on the campus as lessees, we were not allowed to have a sign out with our church name. We were not allowed to utilize what they described as their "sacred space" (a literal worship area/room outside of their new sanctuary, formerly their old worship space) to hold worship. We were instead offered a classroom space in their former school building that could be transformed into a makeshift sanctuary (an option we accepted).

Now, as we approach two years together, it appears whatever fears were brewing have been allayed. Although we remain in the school building classroom, the parish has purchased a sign for our church and affixed it to the building. Additionally, we have begun the process of planning several collaborative outreach efforts. Members from both congregations volunteered to work together to lead various committees. We worked together to prepare a Mother's Day Community Meal for approximately two hundred families. We also planned and held a joint Vacation Bible School. While things were not perfect (the parish sent teachers but none of their children or adult students, causing our teachers and children to feel "some kinda way"), it was an attempt to do a new thing. We are still trying to learn, appreciate, and accept one another.

Although we remain two separate denominations and congregations, there are two critical principles I think we can learn from this newly forming relationship.

(1) **Space and time are important.** People need time to observe one another, have discussions about possibilities, and involve each other in decisions. If things don't meld together immediately, avoid jumping to conclusions and becoming overly offended.

Remember that perceptions and former experiences take time to unpack and overcome. Prayerfully discern a good time to explore questions about why something may or may not have worked. During or immediately after the event may not always be the best time. Space and time can give those involved the opportunity to reflect and reconsider their actions and attitudes.

(2) **Emphasize commonalities and respectfully minimize differences.** Indeed we are different. At times, differences are to be celebrated with respect, open minds, and wonder. Differences present great opportunities for learning and growing. Embracing our differences can expand our worldview. At other times, we must minimize our differences. Collaborative work requires this action. Certainly we have differences that cannot be ignored. But what unites us is greater than what divides us. In our case, we desire to reach out to our community and help those in need. We have a common belief in and love for Jesus Christ. We are both relatively small churches and could use more hands and feet to do greater works. We are better together!

Retrospectively, I realize that we (the congregation and I) were naïve about the work that was necessary to build a healthy intercultural congregation. While racism was a major factor and may not have been allayed by workshops and seminars, had we sought more direction and support to address the issues, the outcome may have been different.

Challenges of Maintaining Intercultural Ministry

Historical relationships, societal influences, stereotypes and preconceived notions, power structures, and racial privilege must not be underestimated. Truth telling and depth level/root causes must be acknowledged, examined, processed, and addressed if true intercultural ministries are to develop and thrive.

To this point, I have focused primarily upon my own intercultural context, dealing with Euro-American and African American people. However, another congregation in our region has wrestled with doing intercultural ministry as they received an influx of Karen families from Burma. The majority of the new families do not speak English. Together, they have worked to learn each other's language, customs, and culture. Members from the congregation have shared: "It's not been easy . . . It can be very messy! Their concept of time is different than ours. They change phone numbers regularly. They don't identify themselves using last names, so it can be difficult to figure out family units. We are still figuring things out." The key seems to be an openness and willingness on both parts.

Another reality facing the potential architects of intercultural churches is the racial tensions and systems that are very much present in the United States. Recently, I attended the Conference of National Black Churches (CNBC) Consultation, held in Charleston, South Carolina. The theme of the consultation was "The Healing of Our Nation: Race and Reconciliation." Charleston was chosen as the site for the consultation because of the racial tensions magnified there by the massacre of nine African Americans by a white man during a prayer meeting and Bible study.

Representatives from eight historically African American denominations were present, as well as individuals from historically Euro-American denominations. Participants wrestled with the role of the church in racial reconciliation and healing. It was determined that conciliation has to happen before reconciliation is possible. The legal definition of "conciliation" is "the amicable resolution of a dispute," usually facilitated by a neutral third party, who assists in finding a way to settle the dispute.

One of the consultation presenters, Dr. Camara Phyllis Jones, a Research Director for Centers for Disease Control and Prevention, declared, "Racism is a system of power, structuring opportunity and assigning value based on the social interpretation of how one looks."

Germane to our discussion regarding the challenges and difficulties of doing and maintaining ministry within an intercultural context are Dr.

Jones's phrases: "a system of power," "assigning value," and "social interpretations." Even in the church, power systems, value assignments, and social interpretations do happen based upon how one looks. Because of the tortured and horrific history between Euro-Americans and African Americans as a result of slavery, other minority groups are frequently more readily accepted and embraced in intercultural situations. Even Africans from the Mother Land appear to gain more rapid acceptance than those black individuals born and bred in America.

In my own church context, the same individuals who gladly went on missions trips to Africa, brought back gifts of woven baskets from humble and poor villages, and posted pictures on our sanctuary walls of our church members arm in arm with members from our sister church in Burundi, Africa, were repulsed by the increase of African Americans in our congregation.

In the movie *The Help,* wealthy white women subjected "the help" (African American maids) to humiliating work conditions, including refusing to allow them to use the in-house restrooms. They were relegated to outhouses because of the white women's fear of catching diseases. Those same white women felt proud as they raised monies to be sent to the hungry children in Liberia.

While the white women had no problem raising money for African people on another continent, they did not see any problem with the way they were debasing the African American women right in their homes. Often racism blinds racists to their hypocrisy. In the movie, the white community enjoyed the food prepared by African American women but refused to allow them to sit at their tables. These issues are critical to the discussion of interculturalism.

Hope on the Horizon

While the past and present remain turbulent and painful regarding race relations and the church, there is hope on the horizon. The Millennials (persons reaching young adulthood around the year

2000) appear to be less concerned about the hue of a person's skin and more interested in the humanity of an individual. According to the Pew Research Center, "Millennials are more ethically and racially diverse then older adults."[1]

Millennials are open to diversity and are more connected with one another. The qualities Millennials possess, combined with the power of the gospel, will no doubt change the landscape and outlook of the church. The church by necessity must become intercultural. Young people will demand it. Churches that refuse to embrace individuals of varying cultures and races will die.

The United States is becoming more and more diverse. As one minister said, "America is not a melting pot; it is a stew!" Although we have some commonalities as Americans, we come from different places, different perspectives, different social and economic realities, different opportunities, different cultural nuances. We are different. The Christian church in the United States must continue to work at celebrating our differences and working together through our common thread of humanity.

The church must identify and prayerfully seek to dismantle those antiquated mentalities and structures that perpetuate hostilities and divisions. It must work with the younger generation to capture the heart and soul of today's realities. It cannot remain encased in stained glass cathedrals, dusty pews, and irrelevant creeds. It must open its doors, stand upon the truth of the gospel, do justly, love mercy, and walk humbly with God.

With all of these things in mind, it is my belief that through a strong foundation of faith, prayer, openness, strategy, and shared power and responsibility, intercultural churches will advance racial equality, justice, and reconciliation. Below are some ideas that can help the process.

Biblical and Current Models of Intercultural Churches

The first New Testament church was intercultural. The writer of Acts emphasized that on the day of Pentecost, everyone spoke and heard others in their own language and there was under-standing. "They were all with one accord in one place" (Act 2:1, NKJV). The miracle is still astounding today—when people of dif-ferent languages, both linguistically and culturally, can hear and understand one another. They were not able to do this on their own. This was accomplished by the power of the Holy Spirit after they intentionally spent time together, praying for one another and seeking God.

Successful current-day intercultural churches follow the same process—spending time together, praying in one accord, and seek-ing the Holy Spirit. Each voice is respected. During the CNBC Consultation, some of the most powerful discussions happened during cross-cultural and cross-denominational open dialogues about fears, misconceptions, and the sharing of racial myths and generational perceptions. As we shared, laughed, cried, and gasped, illumination filled the air and a ray of hope appeared.

Dialogue Is Important, But Systemic Strategies Are Critical

Without the changing of systems that perpetuate poverty, igno-rance, economic and educational oppression, health care dispari-ties, and other injustices, the church and the larger society will remain unchanged. The church must determine to engage deeply in community outreach, education, and legislative processes that will change unjust systems in the United States.

Churches are filled with people whose lives are shaped by these unjust systems. In *Church on Purpose: Reinventing Discipleship, Community, and Justice*, Adam L. Bond and Laura Mariko Cheifetz address this issue. In chapter 1, Bond declares:

> What does it mean to be a citizen of God's kingdom and a cit-izen of this country, of the world? These questions are too rel-evant and pressing to avoid them in our churches. As church, we teeter on the verge of irrelevance when we refuse to offer

responsible "God talk" that interrogates our responsibilities as residents of the world.[2]

The church cannot ignore the realities of life circumstances.

Have Open and Honest Conversations

To reach the place of being in one accord, individuals must be prepared to be honest about their thoughts. Have open conversations about people's individual questions, hopes, dreams, fears, and hesitancies. Truths must be spoken in love. Even if it is difficult and uncomfortable, it is better to flesh out differences and concerns at the beginning than to wear masks and pretend that all is well when people really want to scream.

Invite an outside facilitator to come in early in the process—someone who can objectively guide dialogue. Oftentimes we are too close to the situation to see pitfalls and roadblocks. A skilled, godly facilitator could help a congregation to come to terms with the struggles they are facing and identify clear paths toward realizing specific goals. By involving an outside, unbiased resource, a congregation can increase the possibility of receptivity of observations made and suggestions given.

Founder and CEO of J. G. Ebersole Associates and the Renaissance Group, J. Glenn Ebersol Jr., states the benefits an outside, professional facilitator can bring to an organization: unbiased objectivity; increased probability of a successful outcome; outside-the-box thinking; greater buy-in and implementation from team members; elimination of personal agendas; completion of meeting and achievement of desired outcomes in a timely manner; raising issues that need to be raised; creating a safe, nonthreatening environment for open discussion and helping participants feel less intimidated.[3] Although these suggestions were developed for secular organizations, these observations ring true for any organization.

Share Positions of Power

Healthy intercultural churches have various ethnicities represented in the pew *and* in positions of power. Frequently, churches with cosmetic diversity have tokens or a few people of color on boards with little or no influence. They tout having diversity. However, if those in positions have no voice, power, or influence, they are merely shadows. All ethnicities represented in the church should be evident throughout the life of the church—in leadership structures, governing documents, worship, music, fellowship, outreach, and all programs. Intercultural churches happen best when people from the diverse cultures participate in shaping and forming the activities of the church. When those in the dominant culture make decisions without input from the other ethnicities, they run the risk of offending and alienating those they may be trying to include.

An excellent online website, "Intercultural Church," shares the following about a healthy intercultural perspective:

> The church's embrace of interculturalism comes from an understanding that humanity is complete only when it embraces the full diversity that our creative God placed into the cultures of the world. "No individual alone, and no people group alone, can fully understand God," suggests pastor and professor Randy Woodley. "But working together, uniting our many different experiences, cultures, and understandings, we can see more of the greatness of God." Part of a congregation's new, intercultural identity is not just tolerating our differences, but embracing, celebrating, guarding, and defending our differences.[4]

Be Prepared to Go the Distance

Even under the best of circumstances, blending cultures can be challenging. This is not for the faint of heart! A congregation must be committed to doing the hard work necessary for the intercultural ministry to flow. Those who want quick fixes and immediate con-gealing will be disappointed. Even if it appears to happen quickly, beneath the surface there will always be challenges. The reward for intentionality and prayerful strategizing, however, will be the sweet aroma of togetherness, unity, and love. Giving birth is always painful and laborious, but the beauty of that which comes forth always trumps the struggle. The intercultural church is the true rep-resentation of heaven on earth.

Notes
1. Pew Research Center, "Millennials: Confident. Connected. Open to Change," Executive Summary, February 24, 2010.
2. Adam L. Bond and Laura Mariko Cheifetz, eds., *Church on Purpose: Reinventing Discipleship, Community, and Justice* (Valley Forge, PA: Judson Press, 2015), 11.
3. J. Glenn Ebersole Jr., "Ten Powerful Benefits from Using a Professional Outside Facilitator According to Your Strategic Thinking Business Coach," accessed March 30, 2016, http://www.evancarmichael.com/library/glenn-eber-sole/Ten-Powerful-Benefits-From-Using-A-Professional-Outside-Facilitator-According-To-Your-Strategic-Thinking-Business-Coach.html.
4. Intercultural Church, accessed March 30, 2016, http://interculturalchurch.com/narrative/introduction/.

CHAPTER 9

Just Power

Ten Principles for Building Intercultural Leadership Teams

Rev. Dr. Daniel Hill

The theme of this book—establishing intercultural ministries—is one painted throughout the pages of the early church's origin story. As Luke explored this possibility in his Acts of the Apostles, he seemed captured by the question of whether the church of Jesus Christ could move beyond the racial confines of its Jewish origins and grow into a proliferation of intercultural communities of faith.

Luke's early writings show a clear fascination with the vision. In Acts 1 he paid close attention to the breadth of nations represented in Jesus' marching orders to the disciples. In Acts 2 he carefully notated the presence of each individual nation as the Spirit exploded upon the early believers at Pentecost. And in Acts 4 he demonstrated the impact of the unity experienced by the early Christians as they pooled their resources to provide collectively for the poor among them.

What seemed most to captivate Luke's interest when it came to the establishment of intercultural communities was the notion of power. Luke intuitively understood what any of us who work with intercultural organizations do: that when different cultural groups unite together, the most critical dynamic revolves around how power is shared. Questions immediately arise: How are decisions made? Who makes them? Whose voices get heard in the process? How do those voices get heard? Whose stories get told? How do resources get released?

As Luke observed the buzz associated with the establishment of the early church, perhaps he also watched to see if issues of power would erupt. Only a little while after the dawn of the church, a racial-cultural power issue flared, as recorded in Acts 6.

In a spirit of caring for the vulnerable, the apostles had instituted a food-sharing program for the widows of the community. The program served widows of two different cultural backgrounds, and they were having very different experiences with the food giveaway (Acts 6:1). The first group of widows was of Hebrew origin, and as such they had direct access to the church's dominant culture of the time. The second group was of Grecian origin, but they felt that their outsider status was resulting in marginalization.

Based on the way he tells the story, it seems that Luke wondered how the early church would respond. Would they be open enough to perceive this as a power issue? Or would they be dismissive of the complaints? Whichever path they chose was going to set a trajectory for the church in regards to its intercultural competency.

The apostles recognized that there were important issues of power at play, and they crafted a structural solution that responded accordingly. They empowered the group most affected by the problem to solve their own problem and created a pathway for leaders in the marginalized group to emerge (Acts 6:3-7). It was both effective and honoring of everyone in the community.

But as important as this display of shared power was, it remained only a preview of what was to come. The movement of Jesus Christ was about to take root in the global city of Antioch, and the world was about to witness the formation of an urban, intercultural church led by a group of diverse pastors, teachers, and prophets who shared power in their leadership.

Plurality of Power in Antioch

Antioch played a major role in the New Testament church. It was a port city and transportation hub, and therefore attracted all kinds of people. It was the third-largest city in the Roman Empire, but it was by far the most culturally diverse: Greeks, Syrians, Phoenicians, Jews, Arabs, Persians, Italians, and various residents from Africa were all part of the city's cosmopolitan mix.[1]

The presence of such a wide spectrum of nationalities created lots of social friction. In *The Rise of Christianity*, Rodney Stark sketches a portrait of Antioch as a city so fragmented that it was divided into eighteen separate ethnic quarters.[2] From a human perspective, Antioch was an odd location for a small band of culturally homogenous Christ followers to root the nucleus of their movement.

Yet this is exactly where Luke perceived the full power of the resurrected Christ realized. The church in Antioch not only transformed the city where it was located but also became the mother church for every future faith community in the New Testament.

There is much that could be explored within the church of Antioch, but for the purposes of this chapter I will focus on the single word *power*. What made the church of Antioch so unique was that it was led by a plurality of culturally diverse leaders.

Luke lists the leadership team by name in Acts 13:1: first was Simeon called Niger, who was from sub-Saharan West Africa. Next was Lucius from Cyrene, a city near the northern coast of Africa. Third was Manaen of Palestine, who also had the backroom power politics of Rome on his résumé. Fourth was Saul, a European-trained Jew from Asia Minor. And then there was the ringleader and architect of the group, Barnabus from Cyprus (Acts 4:32).

Luke wants us to pay close attention to this remarkable achievement. The most important church in the New Testament became the model for intercultural churches. A team of five pastors, teachers, and prophets from three continents shared leadership and power. It's no wonder that this was the first place that the word *Christian* was used (Acts 11:26).

The significance of what happened in Antioch is hard to overstate for those of us who long to build authentically intercultural communities today. Small strides such as diversifying the faces in the worship band or on the hospitality team can be positive steps for a church that wants to move in this direction. But Antioch pushes us to mature our thinking beyond superficial expressions of cosmetic diversity. We must tackle the dynamic of power.

Principles for Justly Sharing Power

For the remainder of this chapter, I would like to share some principles for developing and deepening culturally diverse leadership teams that share power. These principles emerge from many years of working together with others in River City Community Church, the congregation I planted in January 2003.

First, a brief bit of background on our context. The church is located in the Humboldt Park neighborhood of Chicago, a historic beacon for low-to-moderate-income residents and immigrants. It is a mixed community, with Puerto Ricans traditionally populating the east and African Americans populating the west end of the neighborhood. Its central location (less than three miles west of the downtown area) has led to a recent wave of both young professionals and Mexican immigrants, further diversifying the neighborhood.

River City Community Church's vision is to become a multiethnic community of Jesus followers who transform our city through worship, reconciliation, and neighborhood development. As such, we have a strong, historical commitment to being an intercultural community of faith. We have worked hard to develop and deepen a leadership team that shares power. And though the team experiences transitions from time to time, we have developed a sustained track record that reflects cultural and gender diversity.

Here are ten principles that have emerged from our journey.

Principle 1: Embrace a Team Leadership Model
I put this principle first because my experience suggests that team leadership is an unusual proposition for most congregants. Each

individual has a culturally formed understanding of leadership, yet few of these embrace team leadership as a normative model.

For instance, in my upbringing the ideal leader was seen as synonymous with a corporate CEO. He or she was a person of vision and had strong ideals that pushed toward that desired reality. He or she was resolute in moving the congregation there and would let nothing stand in the way of getting to the hoped-for destination.

That particular leadership model that I was exposed to is just one of many. Some congregants are groomed to search for a Moses figure—an iconic leader who hears directly from God and then translates a vision for the people who will faithfully follow. Other congregants have been formed in authoritarian environments where there is a strong leader figure who is never challenged.

There are many more variations of leadership styles, but naming or critiquing those is not my main point. I'm simply trying to highlight the important reality that most people have been groomed to think of leadership in a mold that is quite different from the team leadership model. Serving together within a team context is a big cultural shift, both for the leaders and for those who are part of the organization. Like any culture shift, it has to be named, explored, taught, and evaluated.

Principle 2: Create an Environment Where Leaders Come Fully as They Are

This principle strikes me as being simultaneously the most obvious *and* the most difficult. It's obvious in the sense that if a culturally diverse team is going to be built, then each person must own and embrace his or her own cultural identity. And yet, in reality, that is far more difficult to put into practice than it is to state in theory.

For example, some members of the leadership team may have been shaped by a culture that values speaking quietly and discourages the overt expression of potentially charged emotions like anger and grief. Other members will come from cultural environments where highly emotive and expressive responses are the norm.

And then on top of that, there is always the elephant in the room of white power and privilege. Team members who have come of age in the dominant, white culture will interact with the world differently from the way that those who are part of groups with a history of oppression and trauma will interact.

There is no way to create an environment where leaders come fully as they are without addressing and exploring these cultural dynamics head on. Diverse team members are going to represent very different collective histories, and these differences must be analyzed and embraced. The team needs to be on the lookout for which individuals feel free to speak and which shrink away; who is quick to answer a question and who is slow.

In Christ, we each have the freedom to bring our best selves to the table. But in Christ we also explore the historical dynamics of power and privilege that have shaped our backgrounds, and we conscientiously work to cultivate a different kind of atmosphere than the ones we've all come to know in the everyday world.

Principle 3: Establish a Consensus-Based Approach to Decision Making

I would contend that you cannot fully implement the second principle without tying it into this one. One of the potentially frustrating dynamics of serving together in an intercultural setting is determining how a debated topic moves from stimulating conversation to a final decision. There is often a wide gulf between those two. It is therefore important that each leadership team gets clear on the protocol for how they will make decisions together.

In our setting, we have agreed that all major decisions must be unanimous. It was a bit scary to land on this approach, because it leaves the door open for gridlock when we can't all agree. But the alternative seemed even scarier to us, and making decisions based on a majority vote would leave us unnecessarily vulnerable in our setting.

There are a couple of caveats that enable us to embrace this model of decision making. We recognize that for an environment to be created in which each team member brings his or her full self, there are bound to be differences of opinion. It's virtually impossible to equally align every person's perspective on every issue.

So how do you find unanimity when there is a multitude of perspectives? I'll mention three commitments within our protocol to enable us to make decisions unanimously:

1. We strongly encourage everyone to voice her or his opinion on an issue, and we leave ample time for discussion and debate. Often the debate is intense enough that it requires multiple meetings before we've hashed it through. It does make the decision process appear slow to the rest of the congregation at times, and that does have to be addressed. Because we value this process, however, we explain the seeming delay to our congregation so that they can understand this unique but important dynamic of power sharing.

2. We commit to one another to handle any conflict that arises in these debates in a healthy way (more on that in the next principle).

3. We recognize that we are part of a diverse team, with diverse perspectives, and that there are times when some of us need to defer to the wider group. Deferring, at least as we define it, is very different from capitulating to the dominant view. We would never violate a team member's personal convictions on an issue. If he or she feels strongly about something, we will stay there until the matter is resolved. However, we also recognize the important nuance that distinguishes a personal, uncompromising conviction from a passionate perspective that may not be in alignment with the group consensus. Part of being in a team is recognizing that there are times when group wisdom needs to trump individual opinion, and we have all taken turns deferring in instances like that.

Principle 4: Mutually Commit to Authentic Conflict Resolution

I had a mentor in my twenties who would say, "If you haven't said sorry to someone in the last week, then you are probably not living in authentic community." That wisdom was conveyed in the midst of a culturally homogenous community. How much truer must it be when living in an intercultural one?

It's impossible to avoid conflict in authentic intercultural communities. If we come as our full selves and express opinions passionately, conflict will naturally arise. Instead of avoiding the inevitable presence of conflict, we should expect and embrace it.

Our shared axiom is "keeping short accounts." We promise to avoid letting any hurt feelings fester. If there's even a chance that a wedge has been formed through a passionate interaction or accidental comment, it will be addressed immediately.

Principle 5: Remain on the Lookout for Tokenism

This principle is especially important for churches that have a strong white presence in the congregation. There will be times when, in the name of diversity, a hasty attempt is made to add a member to the team that is from a non-majority culture. While any attempt in this direction is generally a positive step, we must also remain acutely aware of the dangers of tokenism.

Wikipedia defines tokenism as "the policy and practice of making a perfunctory gesture towards the inclusion of members of minority groups. The effort of including a token employee to a workforce usually is intended to create the appearance of social inclusiveness and diversity."[3] Webster's defines tokenism as "the policy or practice of making only a symbolic effort."[4]

How do you differentiate between intentional diversification of a team and tokenism? The most straightforward way to begin the process is to ask. The key factor is the degree of agency that all team members feel. Do they feel that their presence is valued? Do they feel that they are allowed and encouraged to speak up when they have an opinion? Do they feel that they are bringing their full selves to the team? Do they feel that they have power within the context of the team? Do they fear that they will be seen as an impediment if they share a contrarian perspective?

Principle 6: Be Mindful of the Acts 6 Model

I alluded to Acts 6 earlier in this chapter and remain convinced that it contributes an important principle to the task of building leadership teams that share power. What the apostles experienced there is very common; they launched a program with good intentions that was designed to support a vulnerable population. But good intentions weren't enough, and in launching the program they created a dynamic where one of the groups felt marginalized.

This becomes a key dynamic for each intercultural congregation as well. Even when the motives of leadership are pure, it won't change the fact that some groups will feel marginalized by the collective decisions that are made. Instead of viewing this as a threat, it should be embraced as an opportunity. The unrest by vulnerable groups in the congregation creates the capacity for deeper engagement by all involved parties.

It's significant that when this happened in Acts 6, the leadership team didn't make a decision for the marginalized group. Too often we make the mistake of doing the opposite.

Whenever a dominant culture selects leaders without input, it sets the stage for tokenism. Questions naturally arise like, "How did this person become a leader? Who decided that they should represent us?"

The apostles set a great precedent for each of us to follow. They go to the group who is feeling marginalized and invite them to nominate leaders from within their community to solve the problems that they are facing. This is a brilliant way to share power and raise up a new generation of indigenous leaders.

Principle 7: Emphasize the Importance of Solving Problems Together

In the early days of planting River City, I was overwhelmed with the amount of culturally loaded challenges I was facing. In a desperate search for wisdom, I began searching for diverse mentors outside of the church. There were some seasoned veterans who offered to guide me during this critical season, and I'll be forever grateful to them. But they also made it clear that I needed to make a shift in my approach if River City was going to continue in its journey of becoming an authentically intercultural church.

One of my mentors was the pastor of an intercultural church in the Bahamas, and he summed it up perfectly: "Daniel, I know you are facing lots of challenges, and you are sincerely searching for wisdom in how to negotiate those, and that's all good. But you need to also realize that your community will remain in a limited state for as long as you are relying on mentors from the outside. You must push forward to the formation of a leadership team within your own community. It's not just the answers that are important—it's the process of *how* you get to the answers. There is no substitute for prayerfully wrestling through these issues . . . *together*."

That was one of the most important pieces of advice I received as a church planter. I am more aware than ever of the major challenges facing our church, but I no longer feel the pressure to figure those out on my own. One of the things I most look forward to on a weekly basis is doing collective, cross-cultural problem solving. It's spiritually enriching, intellectually stimulating, and functionally critical as we solve problems together.

Principle 8: Submit to a Common Vision

One of the missteps I made in my earlier attempts at intercultural team building was to underemphasize the need to be bound to each other, and to God, by a common vision. I discovered that I was capable of recruiting smart, strong-minded people to join my leadership team, and even to get them to bring their full selves to the table. And yet, when we didn't have some agreed-upon, higher goal that we were moving toward, we ended up going in circles.

Every organization and faith community must have a sense of vision—a picture of where they believe God is leading them. In our setting, this vision revolves around the three pillars of worship, reconciliation, and neighborhood development. We often have spirited debate about what it means to fully actualize all of those, but the vision itself is not in question. This vision is what creates a foundation for us as we chart a collective course together.

Principle 9: Develop a Set of Values That Adheres the Leadership Team Together

As a white pastor, it is critical that I lead with a high degree of cultural self-awareness. I have needed to learn how to balance a pair of tricky realities. On one hand, I have innumerable blind spots that have been formed by the dominant culture I grew up in, and I need to be relentless about identifying those. On the other hand, I also fell into a pattern of being paralyzed by my fear of cultural blind spots and correspondingly struggled to articulate any clear sense of expectation for the leaders who served in our ministry.

Dr. Brenda Salter McNeil, one of the key mentors for our church, encouraged our pastoral team to spell out clearly values that would undergird our leadership—values that would be nonnegotiable for men and women of all cultural backgrounds.

This delineation of values became a priceless exercise for us, enabling us to create common vocabulary for what we expected of each other. It also became critical for the recruitment and development of future leaders.

We have seven core values that shape the ethos of our leadership culture:

1. Humble – The Bible is abundantly clear that God opposes the proud and lifts up the humble, and this truth cuts across every

cultural and economic background. A posture of humility must shape how all leaders serve our body.

2. Hungry – Many social agendas come into play when you attempt to build an intercultural community. Hunger for God and God's kin-dom must underscore all of the human efforts. "Blessed are those who hunger and thirst for righteousness and justice, for they will be filled" (Matthew 5:6, adapted).

3. Smart – Cross-cultural environments are complicated, and we all need to be learning, all the time. We want to have a culture that embraces risk and accepts failure. We want to be smart enough to avoid making the same mistakes over and over again.

4. Emotionally healthy – Emotional health is particularly important in cross-cultural environments, where past traumas will be triggered on a regular basis. Leaders must be self-aware enough to name their pain, anger, and sadness and then find the resources to help them process those emotions.

5. Cross-culturally concerned – Our leaders need to have not only the skills to operate cross-culturally but also the motivation to be concerned for other groups. We are a family, and each part of the body needs to be concerned with the other parts.

6. Team-centric – We tend to celebrate team victories much more than individual victories, even though each individual is important and honored. And when it comes to paid staff, we emphasize that each position is interdependent with the others. It's part of an overall belief that the collective representation of the team is what makes the biggest impact.

7. Hope-driven – In Zechariah 9:12 the people of God are referred to as "prisoners of hope," and this is part of our leadership identity. There is much wrong with the world, and in a spirit of prophetic challenge, these wrongs must be called out. But we are prisoners of hope. We must continually follow the Spirit in the pursuit of God's will to be done, on earth as it is in heaven.

Principle 10: Cultivate an Atmosphere of Love

First Corinthians 13 reminds us in no uncertain terms that nothing matters at the end of the day but love. We can speak in the tongues of angels, fathom all mysteries, move mountains, and give away everything we have to the poor, but we have gained nothing if we don't have love. Love is the motivation of God, as expressed in Jesus. Love is the end to which God is taking us all.

Love is that which allows us to be patient with each other, to honor each other, and to keep no record of wrongs. Love rejoices with truth, protects each other, and always trusts. Love must be the driving factor behind everything we do.

I put this one last, because it is what undergirds every one of these principles. We must learn to love and trust each other, love and trust God, and love and trust our congregation. The legendary Dr. John Perkins, founder of Christian Community Development Association (CCDA), says it succinctly with the title of his autobiography: *Love Is the Final Fight.*[5]

In summary, the locus of intercultural transformation revolves around the navigation of power. Each congregation needs to develop a plan for how it will explore historical power dynamics and implement a system for sharing power across diverse constituencies. I pray that some of these ten principles delineated in this chapter may serve as a catalyst for those conversations.

Notes

1. Jeff Iorg, *The Case for Antioch: A Biblical Model for a Transformational Church* (Nashville: B&H Publishing Group, 2011), 15.

2. Rodney Stark, *The Rise of Christianity* (Princeton, NJ: Princeton University Press, 1996), 157–58.

3. Accessed November 16, 2016, https://en.wikipedia.org/wiki/Tokenism.

4. Accessed November 16, 2016, http://www.merriam-webster.com/dictionary /tokenism.

5. John M. Perkins, *Love is the Final Fight* (Ventura, CA: Regal Books, 2010).

CHAPTER 10

Equals at the Table

Angie Hong

Whenever I think about the Holy Spirit pouring out over the masses at Pentecost, I vividly imagine the diverse groups of people from all of Jerusalem being transformed by the power of the triune God in corporate worship. In that supernatural moment, hearts and minds were fully alive, allowing the believers to lay down their vulnerable selves in the presence of God and one another in unity. Even more amazing were the ways in which the believers daily lived in this transformed reality as they worshiped together daily and met each others' needs in tangible ways as a united Christian community.

This biblical vision of Jewish and Gentile believers in an inclusive worshiping community should help sustain diverse and intercultural Christian communities today. When God called me away from my primarily monoethnic church upbringing to step into a vision of a multiethnic church in Durham, North Carolina, I dared to believe that a Christ-transformed community of people from all nations as described at Pentecost was possible. I was ecstatic and eager to participate in this kind of ministry, and I went on a quest to seek wisdom and knowledge from the many communities who went before me.

What I found in reality was quite different. As if personal and interpersonal brokenness and sin weren't enough to struggle with as Christians, churches today remain the most segregated organizations that exist, more than any other institution in America.[1] Racism, which divides society in order to keep dominant power structures intact, has taken deep roots in the church in ways that are subtle, hidden, and twisted. Instead of inclusive and countercultural communities, there exist highly exclusive, business-as-usual spirituality clubs or spiritless social justice groups. The churches I found that did offer wisdom were, in fact, relatively young, and struggling in their efforts to make diverse intercultural congregations. Other churches that had a longer existence as diverse congregations had leadership that consisted of mostly white males, which seemed inauthentic to me. In other words, the idyllic, supernatural, and transformative Pentecost vision I pictured in my mind seemed almost impossible to achieve in the real world. Almost.

I have seen glimmers of hope in some communities, including my own. But I am no longer naïve about how excruciating this journey can be, as it calls me to be awakened to myself in ways that invoke pain, sacrifice, resurrection, hope, and joy. It calls me to peel back the many armored layers I have built up over the years, sharp edges that have been formed and fortified based on my personal experiences as a minority female in church, as both an ignorant participant and recipient of systemic oppression. But I find hope each Sunday during Communion, as I am reminded that Jesus still invites all of us to covenantal love.

There were three main practices that emerged in shaping the vibrant community at CityWell[2] in Durham to help sustain us in our path toward that marvelous vision: (1) an awakening and recognition of our God-given identities as gifts; (2) deeper and transformative corporate worship; and (3) a calling to engage in justice and reconciliation together.

Gifted as Created

I am a second-generation Korean American woman, born in the United States and raised in the American South. There are many assumptions and expectations of these different parts of my identity, and as I grew up and matured, I noticed how the world viewed most of these parts in a negative light. As a Korean American born in the United States, herein referred to as America, I was considered an outsider in the land I was born in, what Erika Lee refers to as "perpetual foreigners at worst, or probationary Americans at best."[3] The model minority myth has been a challenge unique to the Asian American experience. I did not have many upstanding, respectable, fall-in-line Asian American friends who did exceptionally well in math and science, yet this was the narrow window in which we were expected to fit. Adding the gender complications of being a woman proved to be even more challenging.[4] The stereotype of the Asian female as submissive to the point of subjugation and shunned from having leadership roles or even speaking up in many situations seemed to further seal my fate in society.

As I experienced life as a Southerner, Confederate flags and Confederate culture were a normal part of everyday life. Displaying Southern pride meant preserving a culture of plantation life, drinking and eating the food mostly created by African slaves, and fighting to protect a seemingly noble Civil War heritage, even if it meant normalizing segregation or flying the Confederate flag on lawns and pickup trucks. Many of my friends tote guns of every shape and size even today, not afraid to bring them along on road trips or social functions. Lingering Jim Crow justifications are also felt cementing the walls that separate race and class.

My parents, in order to survive as poor immigrants from Korea with little education, sought community and business networks through the Korean church. Similarly, my second-generation friends and I learned to rely on each other to navigate our primarily white schools and an American culture that clashed in almost every way with that of our parents. In this Korean church community I found belonging and normalcy among my peers with similar narratives. There was no need to assimilate or pretend to laugh off micro aggressions and ignorant bigotry, nor was it assumed that I was automatically gifted in math and science. I was me, and I fit in just as I was. It didn't matter what city I moved to or what denomination I belonged to; as long as there was a Korean church (with a second-generation English ministry), I knew I would find refuge and asylum from the outside world that did not count me as a valid voice.

When God first called me out of the safe haven of my church community into intercultural ministry, I had no idea the degree to which it would be disorienting, shocking, and at times, traumatic. I first chalked it up to clashing personalities and a general resistance to change by the leaders, possibly even generational differences. As other newcomers from the dominant culture joined and were given power and voice, however, I began to sense that it wasn't just my personality or my communication style. Even more disturbing were the subliminal messages coming from those in leadership, as requests to be heard were met with the same roadblocks. I began to feel incredibly discouraged, and I second-guessed myself and my abilities. Was I not smart enough? Were my ideas really that terrible? I wanted to contribute to the church as a leader, but the church confirmed what the world was telling me: I did not have the right gender, race, ethnicity, and geographical location to make an impact in the kin-dom of God.

If I had not left the enclave of my Korean community bubble, I would not have been awakened to such views on who I was and opinions on who God created me to be. I fluctuated between signs of hope and even more signs of discouragement over my calling, resulting in a sort of wilderness period.

Then came another calling to join CityWell, an urban church plant that would be intentionally multiethnic with a focus on the reconciliation of God's people. By this point I had become acquainted with many pastors, mostly white and male, who were excited about the idea of an intercultural church. I had experienced tokenism and marginalization more than I had ever wanted to in my lifetime, and I was highly suspicious of anyone who used the language of reconciliation without concrete action. I proceeded forward into the church plant with caution, building up a mental and emotional wall to protect myself from being vulnerable to harm or rejection. I intentionally made myself an outside observer, watching out for the same methods of implicit bias I had experienced before.

Sure enough, there were many initial mistakes made by the pastor and the leadership team at CityWell. And yet, something was different about this pastor and leadership team in the ways they took seriously the call to bring the Acts 2 vision to life. The emphasis on realizing and seeking out the gifts of each person and group in the community and building trusting relationships in which to struggle, fail, and recover began to infuse breath into our community.

I developed a restored hope that breaking down my guarded walls would bring new life in my community and for myself. Despite the fact that the world and past church experiences made parts of my identity seem disruptive and easily dismissed, the CityWell community helped each part be seen as a God-given gift. The fact that I was Korean American added to the richness of my community as people eagerly sought to learn from my narrative, experiences, and gifts I had to contribute from my immigrant church upbringing. The fact that I was a woman serving in a leadership capacity as music minister gave other women in the congregation a sense of representation and voice. As a Southerner, I knew how to empathize with those who grew up in Southern culture and gently enter into dialogue about justice and race with those on multiple sides of cultural and political issues. And as an Asian American female, I sought to bear witness to the fact that Jesus is working in all of us and has a specific place in ministry for people like me.

Transforming Worship

The individual transformation and identity development journeys that I and other CityWell members were experiencing translated to the flourishing of our journeys with one another, making it possible for our hearts to become fully alive together in our gathered worship. We desired realization of the vision in Revelation 21:22-26 (NRSV): "I saw no temple in the city, for its temple is God the Almighty and the Lamb. . . . People will bring into it the glory and the honor of the nations." The nations will not simply be present in the new heaven and new earth; rather, the people would bring "the glory and the honor" of their tribes in full authentic representation. These verses are a powerful reminder that our corporate worship had to reflect the vast diversity of our congregation, the development of postures of humility and deep love for one another, and an intentionality in hearing from those who were marginalized.

I had the privilege of helping to craft the weekly corporate worship gatherings for CityWell as the music minister. I sought out many different kinds of voices at CityWell, asking them to contribute to the formation of worship. What I asked of them was to share all the different parts of their God-given identities with each other and somehow learn to incorporate them into our communal practices.

There was a gradual shift in participation in this process-based ministry and shared leadership within the congregation. The musicians on the worship team, used to keeping their heads down and playing what they were told, were surprised that I wanted to know their histories of playing music in the church and the types of worship music that spoke to them. Congregation members felt ownership in the molding of our worship practices, and I tried my best to listen, facilitate discussion, and incorporate ideas.

There is a term used by health care workers called "cultural humility," defined as the "ability to maintain an interpersonal stance that is other-oriented (or open to the other) in relation to aspects of cultural identity that are most important to the [person]."[5] Whereas cultural "competency" suggests an end product to the amount of knowledge of different cultures, cultural "humility" suggests an ongoing process of self-evaluation and self-critique, and of valuing the diversity of others. In Ephesians Paul addresses this idea of cultural humility to the diverse church, encouraging them to "lead a life worthy of the calling to which you have been called, with all humility and gentleness, with patience, bearing with one another in love, making every effort to maintain the unity of the Spirit in the bond of peace" (Ephesians 4:1-3, NRSV).

I admit to making many mistakes in my presumptions about the cultural background of many people based on appearance or ethnicity. For instance, I assumed that most African Americans prefer gospel music to all other types of worship music. This, in fact, was not true, and I realized how limited my imagination was in my assumptions. I wondered in what other ways I limited the preferences or capabilities of others based on skin color or cultural background. Through these awakenings, I learned to value each individual, her or his cultural background, and heartfelt expressions of worship.

I also realized that intentional conversations needed to be facilitated for groups that were easily marginalized. One such group consisted of individuals with developmental disabilities. Many barriers to inclusive corporate worship were named and fleshed out by these individuals and advocates during our general discussions, including reading literacy, ease of songs sung, noise level, and attention span. We discussed these barriers and hoped to welcome feedback and suggestions. As a result, we incorporated simple choruses in American Sign Language, provided "fidgets" or self-regulating tools meant to aid with attention and active listening during sermons or announcement times, and invited individuals to help in leadership as part of the worship team or the communion serving team. By creating quarterly check-ins to gather feedback and discuss more strategies to implement from this group, we continue to press on in the spirit of Christian humility, valuing others, and adding to the richness and scope of our worship.

Since there were so many cultures that clashed both in values and preferences, not all discussions and interactions were positive or welcomed. For instance, people raised objections to singing songs in different languages, especially more difficult songs with complicated lyrics, and we had numerous heated discussions of the nature and length of our testimony times. Another example is the value and organization of time. I, as a linear thinker and organizer, feel great embarrassment if I am late to a meeting. I identify this feeling as a mixture of my type-A personality and my cultural ties to the Confucian values of hierarchy and respect for authority. I try my best to slip into the room unnoticed and make as little interruption as possible to the meeting that has already begun. By contrast, a friend of mine in ministry is a very circular thinker with a different concept of time, coming from a mixture of his gregarious personality and cultural Mexican ties to being hospitable. He would arrive late to the same meeting, greeting everyone by name with a big hug and engaging in some small talk before settling into his seat. His actions infuriated me, as I thought they were disrespectful of others' time and disruptive to the meeting. Similarly, my actions infuriated him, as he thought they were rude and cold toward the others in the meeting. As we engaged in our community together we learned to be honest with each other on the dynamics of these situations.

Imagine these same dynamics playing out in the following scenarios when it comes to clashing intercultural values: childcare/nursery, youth group, sex, sexuality, gender, food, and politics, just to name a few. In some cultures, etiquette claims that some of these topics are too taboo to discuss. But as Paul describes in Ephesians, all are opportunities to practice postures of humility and listening, forging new paths together in covenantal relationship.

I hold in ever-present tension authentic worship on a personal and vulnerable level, and space for others to worship on a personal and vulnerable level. Corporate worship in a church setting serves as a celebration, recognition, and confession of ourselves and our identities; there is no limit to the creativity and complex beauty of how this worship is expressed.

Justice and Reconciliation

When we have a strong sense of identity in worship practices, we learn to embody the "we" in the Divine Love, and the work of justice and reconciliation is possible. The realities of our structural divides still exist, but the transformative power of Christ beckons us to examine the worldly power and the oppressive systems that seek to keep us apart. Listening in our worshiping communities, both to each other's personal struggles and to the larger systemic injustices that exist to perpetuate separation, is a radical act of reconciliation. We must realize that breaking down barriers requires not a simple bridge but a giant wrecking ball, and we must engage in this work together.

One such example is our community's response to a member who was deported to Mexico with his wife and three young children. In the months leading up to his deportation, we rallied around him and his family in prayer that his visa application would be approved. We then threw a benefit concert with him, raising an entire year's salary for a potential local job that would allow him to stay in the United States. When he was told that his visa application was denied and that he had only one week to pack up everything and leave, we became advocates for him by learning more about immigration laws and reform, becoming informed activists on these matters.

Another example is more personal. Along with being marginalized as a Korean American woman, I also realized that my parents, in order to survive and live the American dream, engaged in racist business practices to make money and provide for their kids. They racially profiled each applicant who applied for jobs at their businesses. They paid their workers close to minimum wage, and the women were always paid less than the men. As their child, I bene-fited directly from these injustices. By identifying this unspoken nar-rative of my power and privilege and sharing my power with oth-ers, I sought justice for oppressed people in our community: "For you were called to freedom, brothers and sisters; only do not use your freedom as an opportunity for self-indulgence, but through love become slaves to one another" (Galatians 5:13, NRSV).

Fully Present, Fully Guests, Fully at the Table

A thriving intercultural ministry, though aesthetically beautiful in appearance, requires countercultural and radical practices. Many churches and communities fail to recognize the scope of work involved, with all its richness and complexities. By affirming one another's identity as God's gift to community, engaging regularly in transformational worship together, and understanding each other in a spirit of intercultural humility in order to advocate for justice and reconciliation, we will discover that the new Jerusalem is not only an idealistic abstract vision, but a beacon of a new reality for the world to see.

Notes

1. LifeWay Research, "American Views on Church Segregation," accessed October 26, 2016, http://lifewayresearch.com/wp-content/uploads/2015/01/American-Views-on-Church-Segregation.pdf.

2. CityWell is a church plant through the United Methodist Church, located in Durham, North Carolina.

3. Erika Lee, *The Making of Asian America: A History* (New York: Simon & Schuster, 2015), 9.

4. PayScale, Inc., "Gender Pay Inequality and Job Type," November 9, 2015, accessed April 22, 2016, http://www.payscale.com/data-packages/gender-pay-gap/job-type.

5. J. N. Hook, D. E. Davis, J. Owen, E. L. Worthington Jr., and S. O. Utsey, "Cultural Humility: Measuring Openness to Culturally Diverse Clients," *Journal of Counseling Psychology* 60, no. 3 (July 2013): 353–60.

PART 3

Future Possibilities
of Intercultural Churches
and Ministries

CHAPTER 11

Ministry at the Margins

Bishop Karen Oliveto

It is Sunday morning in the Tenderloin, a neighborhood in downtown San Francisco. The TL, as it is known, is just a couple of blocks from Union Square, where tourists take selfies in front of cable cars and visit high-end stores, but it feels worlds away: homeless men and women are asleep on the sidewalks, drug deals happen on nearly every street corner, and the stench of human excrement is strong. Yet, every Sunday, visitors from all over the world line up in the Tenderloin neighborhood at the corner of Taylor and Ellis with folks from throughout the Bay Area, waiting for the sanctuary doors of Glide Memorial Church to open for Celebration.

The eight-piece band begins to play and the choir enters singing Douglas Miller's gospel rendition of Fanny Crosby's classic hymn: "Pass me not, O gentle Savior, hear my humble cry; While on others Thou art calling, do not pass me by."[1]

The two lines, "Hear my humble cry" and "Do not pass me by," are punctuated, emphasized by the voices, a plea by those often overlooked to be seen and acknowledged. In the welcome to the gathered community, there is an acknowledgment of this desire.

If you are black, brown, yellow, red, white, or some other beautiful hue of the rainbow, we welcome you here! If you are gay, straight, lesbian, bisexual, transgender, asexual, intersex, queer, questioning, or define who you are and how you love in another way, we welcome you! If you are housed, temporarily sheltered, or homeless, we welcome you! If you are documented or undocumented, we welcome you! If you are Christian, Jewish, Buddhist, Muslim, Hindu, Wiccan, Atheist, or not really sure about spirituality, we welcome you! If you are employed, underemployed, or jobless, we welcome you! If you have fifteen years sobriety or fifteen minutes of sobriety, or perhaps still have a buzz on, you are welcome here! Welcome to this place of unconditional love and unconditional acceptance!

Roots of Diversity: A San Francisco Original

Glide's diversity seems rooted in its DNA, although it wasn't truly realized until the late 1960s. Lizzie Glide (1852–1936), a Sacramento philanthropist who had had a significant religious conversion, noted that San Francisco was one of the least-churched cities in the United States. She created the Glide Foundation to establish and support Glide Memorial Church as a tribute to her late husband. Her hope was that this church (established as a Methodist Episcopal Church, South) could be grounded in a "broad spirit of catholicity in keeping with a vital evangelistic program and message."[2] In 1931, Glide Memorial Church opened its doors. The cornerstone inscription bears witness to Lizzie's intent for the church: *"A House of Prayer for All People, A.D. 1930."*

Glide blossomed into a vibrant congregation whose outreach was felt throughout San Francisco. However, within three decades the church dwindled to fewer than forty members. The Glide Foundation hired Rev. Lewis Durham in 1962 to spend a year considering creative ways the church could embody ministry. After a year, the foundation board opened The Glide Urban Center with the purpose of "(1) training clergy and laity for mission to the city, (2) providing consultative services for urban churches, (3) experimenting in urban ministry, (4) establishing a center on urban life,

(5) supporting specific projects in mission to the city, and (6) providing a team of specialists on the mission to the city."[3] Durham began to assemble a team of clergy for the center and the church, and they began to create ministries in conversation with the Bay Area leaders of the social movements of the 1960s.

Many different groups found Glide to be a place of community. Black Panthers found spiritual nourishment at Glide. Members of the lesbian, gay, bisexual, and transgender (LGBT) community found a safe place at Glide. Hippies, Radical Faeries, anti-war activists, poets, musicians, and artists claimed Glide as their home. Rev. John Moore, a Glide pastor in the early 1960s, noted: "In addition to the kinds of people you see in the church, Glide attracted schizophrenic, euphoric, depressed, and hallucinating people."[4] Glide trustee Laurel Glass put it this way: "We're bringing the Word of God to people who would not otherwise hear it."[5]

Rev. Cecil Williams was hired in 1963 as the minister of evangelism. Williams pushed the edges of the church further still, reaching out to the homeless men and women outside the doors of the church, as well as to sex workers and drug addicts. Glide transformed from a dying urban church with thirty-five elderly white members to an eleven-thousand-member spiritual center that is literally and figuratively the heart of San Francisco.

Williams didn't just invite people in to the church so they could be assimilated into churchy ways. He moved the center of the church to the margins and crafted a theology of liberation with spiritual language as well as ministry programs that began with the real-life, lived realities of those whom society, and even the church, overlook. As Williams described ministry at Glide: "We're taking lonely, alienated, starving, craving people and we're trying to free them to be full human beings."[6]

Anchored by a commitment to unconditional love and unconditional acceptance, congregational life—including worship—took a unique form that was influenced by the San Francisco culture of the 1960s and 1970s. Worship was renamed "Celebration," and music took center stage as professional musicians were recruited from the San Francisco jazz community. The choir, while grounded in gospel music, sang music from a variety of sources, including anti-war movement songs and Motown hits. Dance and poetry were incorporated into Celebration. A large cross which dominated the worship space was removed. Williams felt that the cross, with its prominence in the sanctuary, disempowered people from being agents in their own lives. As Williams explained: "Of course, Christ died for our sins on that cross . . . [but] as long as we allowed racism, homophobia, and other kinds of bigotry to exist, we were still crucifying Jesus on that cross. As long as we crucified Jesus, we did not have to understand why we crucified folks we really despised—any folks who were not like us."[7]

In particular, it was a homeless alcoholic who spoke in Celebration beneath the cross which caused Williams to consider removing the cross:

> To Bart [the homeless man] and a lot of people, the cross was not just a symbol of oppression—it *was*—the oppression. Instead of standing for the unconditional love that Jesus brought to a new community, the cross makes people feel guilty because Jesus died for our sins. And what a crazy concept *that* was: Jesus was crucified for challenging the status quo, for being different, for showing the world how to be accepting and loving of all people.[8]

The following Sunday, Williams preached about the cross:

> See this big cross up here? Well, it is not affirming what it should. The cross should be about giving life, not the taking of life. It should inspire, not belittle. It should reflect the love that Jesus' life brought us, not reject the love and keep us all quiet. The cross

signifies suffering, yes, but it also means a new life coming out of that suffering. And renewing life is what we are about.

So I want you to know that I am going to take this cross down. The cross needs to be among the people, in the streets where the Barts of the world suffer. The church keeps trying to tell us that the cross is here to save humanity. But the truth is, only humanity can save the cross.[9]

The bare wall where the cross once hung quickly became filled with images of people. Long before the use of PowerPoint and LCD projectors, Glide began a light show, utilizing an overhead projector and transparency sheets to show "people embracing, protesting, playing with kids, giving the '60s peace sign, talking to police—just everyday life, joyous and morose, gritty yet life-affirming. . . . And to see humanity *visibly* flowing across the wall where the giant cross used to hang was to feel that God, or whatever spiritual force lived in all of us, became a living force in our lives because we had the eyes to see. We were the cross."[10]

Story of Self, Story of Us

"Seeing images of people like yourself" through the light show, which was and continues to be extremely intentional about including the diversity found at Glide, the TL, San Francisco, and the world, people saw their own reflection, which legitimized their presence in their community and gave them space at Glide, a place to call home. Additionally, the images helped connect people across lines of race, gender, class, sexual orientation, and abilities through their very human, raw content. This diversity is also maintained in the Celebration leaders: pastors, musicians, and choir members are strikingly diverse in race, gender identity, sexual orientation, class, and theology. In addition, each Sunday a member of the community provides the Witness moment in Celebration. Here, too, diverse voices are encouraged to speak the truth of their lives, providing an avenue for connection across lines of difference.

No experience is off-limits at Glide: no act is prohibited from mention, no injustice ignored, no wound too deep to utter. This honesty enables lives that on the surface might seem so different from one's own to be a source of insight that results in deep empathy and connection. It doesn't make us all the same but instead allows connection across the lines of difference.

Core to Glide's theology is "we are all in recovery from something." In other traditions, this might be translated to "we are all sinners." At Glide, the understanding is that across our many identities, there are internal behaviors as well as external systems that hinder us from our full humanity. Our task, as individuals and as community, is to encourage the journey to regaining one's humanity and living it out in beloved community. This is at the heart of how Glide lives into an intercultural community.

Recovery circles, where people gather to engage in Glide's unique form of recovery, include people struggling with addictions of every sort, people healing from emotional wounds, and those who seek to face the indignities and violence of poverty and oppression. These circles are, in many ways, the great equalizer at Glide. If we all are in recovery from something, it means we all require one another's assistance as we seek healing and wholeness.

Glide's recovery model is known as "The Terms of Faith and Resistance." These terms are:

1. I will gain control over my life.
2. I will stop lying.
3. I will be honest with myself.
4. I will accept who I am.
5. I will feel my real feelings.
6. I will feel my pain.
7. I will forgive myself and forgive others.

8. I will rebirth a new life.
9. I will live my spirituality.
10. I will support and love my brothers and sisters.

These terms are spoken at the conclusion of not only recovery circles but also many regular gatherings and meetings of the congregation. They are a reminder of our core expectations as we bring our individual lives into community.

Tensions in Intercultural Ministry

The great diversity that is found at Glide is not without its challenges, however. When the focus of ministry begins with those on the margins—with the lives of those who have been overlooked or oppressed—those who possess privilege find themselves dislocated, no longer at the center themselves. It forces a long hard look into one's privileged status. With this self-examination comes the responsibility to be an agent of change, using one's privilege to change systems and policies that are meant to keep power from others.

This is not easy to do. It creates points of tension when those with privilege are not aware of (or willing to admit) their privilege. It requires the ability to live into and learn from multiple truths. It necessitates constant vigilance. Whose voices are still silenced? Whose lives are still kept in the shadows of the margins? How do we continue to push ourselves and the edges of our community to be open to the forgotten and overlooked?

An example of this tension is found in the #BlackLivesMatter movement at Glide. The Glide community has participated in rallies, held forums, and engaged in actions to highlight the gross injustices experienced by members of the black community—particularly young black men—at the hands of the police. However, within our community are also police officers, good women and men who are as outraged by their colleagues' actions as the rest of the community is. Yet, they often feel attacked and vulnerable when images of the #BlackLivesMatter movement are shown in the light show during Celebrations.

Another issue is how we form groups and points of connection. Creating and maintaining diversity is hard work. It requires both clergy and lay leaders to remain vigilant about how accessible emerging groups and activities are to all members of the community. Are groups being structured in a way that prevents some from joining? Is cost prohibitive to others? It is interesting to note that at Glide, even groups who would seem at first to be more homogenous extend welcome and are open to others who may not fit with the core definition of the group's identity.

A weekly intersection of community occurs at "Speak Out." Speak Out is a time when people in the community openly and safely share their thoughts and feelings. When staff learned that Glide is literally in the middle of the largest population concentration of the formerly incarcerated in the state of California, the first question was, "What should we do?" Then the staff reminded itself of Glide's values and realized that this is the wrong starting point. The question is, "What do the formerly incarcerated say they need?" In order to answer this question, an invitation went out to the neighborhood, seeking the formerly incarcerated, inviting them to a free meal and open mic event. That evening, Freedom Hall was packed, and for one hour, people were invited to share the realities of their lives. This was such an informative and empowering evening that it has become a weekly event. Every Wednesday night, sex workers, staff, addicts, donors, congregants, the housed, and the homeless gather to share their truths.

One evening, a young African American man wove his way to the mic. He swayed before the crowd, his eyes glazed. His teeth and disheveled state told the story of one living on the streets, deep in addiction. The longer he stood silently in front of the crowd, the more the room grew silent. Then he said one sentence: "Can I trust you with my dignity?" With that, he returned to his seat.

Through the expressions of unconditional love and unconditional acceptance, dignity is preserved at Glide. Another Speak Out attendee is May, a Chinese immigrant. May is developmentally disabled and pulls all her possessions behind her in a rolling suitcase. May speaks very little English and what little she speaks is largely unintelligible. However, at every Speak Out, May comes forward and sings. The song is one she has made up and no one can understand the words, but everyone gives her undivided attention. When she ends her song, as people applaud her loudly, she speaks in a strong and clear voice, "I love you all."

Pastor, Power, Privilege

Being a pastor in this setting requires constant self-examination of my own privilege and power. I am a white, educated, middle-class woman who loves another woman. This means I live in the tension of privilege and oppression. As a white person, my race grants me access to places of power and safety that are not readily available to my brothers and sisters of color. I don't worry that by putting on a hoodie, I will be perceived as dangerous. I have never given my nieces and nephews "the talk" about how they should behave if ever stopped by a police officer. I have never been followed in a store by the owner simply because of the color of my skin. I have never had to look very far—in books, movies, television, or church meetings—to see people who look like me. In white America, the color of my skin grants me power and privilege.

However, it is my gender and more specifically my sexual orientation which have put conditions on that power and privilege. As a woman, my voice is not heard with the same authority as that of a man. When I was appointed to Glide Memorial United Methodist Church, I broke the stained glass ceiling of the denomination, becoming the first woman to become senior pastor of one of the top one hundred largest churches within the denomination. Sadly, eight years later, I continue to stand alone as the only woman in that group.

As a woman, my authority and power are seen through the lens of gender bias: how I dress, the tone and timbre of my voice, my hairstyle, make-up, and shoes are all taken into consideration before the content of my character or the substance of my sermon. This bias affects how and even if my message will be heard or my leadership respected.

However, as a lesbian who came out nearly forty years ago, I am aware of the price of oppression and its impact on my life. It was not too many years ago that marriage equality was not even dreamed of as a political possibility. My relationship with another woman was lived in silence, overlooked and ignored in a heteronormative world. I remember what it was like to face the prospect of reserving a hotel room, when one of us would stay in the car so the hotel desk clerk would not know that two women were booking a room with one bed. I recall having to talk about my partner in gender-neutral pronouns and refrain from sharing much of my personal life with colleagues. As a clergywoman in a denomination that prohibits "self-avowed, practicing homosexuals" from ordination, I live with the constant threat of the loss of my ordination and therefore my livelihood, simply because of how I express my love for another human being.

In an intercultural context of ministry like Glide, I consider this tension to be a gift. Knowing the parts of my own life that are marginalized makes me sensitive to the marginalization of others and open to the experiences and expressions of lives so different from my own. As a result, it requires me to confront my own racism— I am an heir of a system that, because of my whiteness, provides me with access and power. That system was built into the very foundations of the United States. As a white person, born and raised in the United States, that propensity to bias is genetically coded through my citizenship. I find myself constantly needing to confess the sin of my racism, to check my own assumptions, biases, and instances when I possess privilege when others don't. I have to continually critique myself and my actions.

A New Lens for Scripture

As the pastor of an intercultural church, I find that my reading of Scripture has been turned on its head as I read through the lens of those on the margins. The voices of the nameless ones in Scripture become more pronounced. The traditional interpretations of familiar passages are no longer acceptable. An example is the passage about "doubting Thomas." Even though many of the disciples tell him Jesus has risen from the grave, Thomas tells them, "Unless I see the nail marks in his hands and put my finger where the nails were, and put my hand into his side, I will not believe" (John 20:25, NIV). It is only when he later encounters the risen Christ and puts his hand in the wounds that he finally believes.

The traditional interpretation of this text is that "blessed are those who have not seen, yet believe." This text becomes problematic when preaching to the marginalized who too often find their reality defined by those with power and privilege. When read from the vantage of the oppressed, Thomas did the faithful act by refusing to let others tell him what his reality ought to be. Thomas becomes a model for personal and communal agency, validating the experiences of those whose lives are discounted.

Bringing the Center to the Margins

Honoring the lives and experiences of those on the margins is key to Glide's success as an intercultural church. Tracy, an African American gay man, has been coming to Glide for nearly two decades. Very effeminate, he moved from Chicago for a more tolerant environment. In the previous churches he attended, he was seen as an embarrassment or abomination and would barely be acknowledged. At Glide, he has an important role each Sunday: bedecked in flashy jewelry (what he calls his "bling"), he vogues his way across the worship platform, modeling Glide items which are for sale after each Celebration. Tracy is not just tolerated but celebrated at Glide. He is invited to bring all that he is into the worship space. This invites us all to bring our whole selves into the space as well.

Tracy also helps produce and star in the largest congregational-life annual fundraiser, "Springlicious." Springlicious features drag kings and queens as well as transfolk in an evening of entertainment. This event brings out all members of the community in support of the performers' efforts. During this night, those whose lives have been lived out of sight become the mainstream and are seen as normative, as all are invited to explore the gifts of gender fluidity.

This is one of many examples of how Glide doesn't just give lip service to diversity. Those on the margins, in particular, provide the building blocks for congregational engagement. It is why Tracy calls Glide "the Disneyland of the Tenderloin . . . because it is a place where dreams really do come true."

The Church's Failure

In a time when the global village is shrinking via technology and social media, the church ought to be in the forefront, modeling to the world ways of living into diversity through intercultural engagement. However, Martin Luther King Jr.'s words continue to echo through the empty pews in our churches: "Sunday morning is the most segregated hour in Christian America." As a sociologist, even I was surprised by a recent Pew Research study that showed my own denomination, The United Methodist Church, to be 94 percent Caucasian within the United States.[11] Further research found that this was based on a relatively small sample, but even the denomination's own data revealed that The United Methodist Church is 89.99 percent Caucasian.[12]

I realize that my social location has a lot to do with the perspective I have on the church. In the annual conference in which I serve, the California-Nevada Annual Conference, Caucasians comprise

65 percent of the membership.[13] United Methodists in this region are diverse in race, ethnicity, language, and sexual orientation. However, while there is diversity at the annual conference level, the local church level tells a different story, with churches frequently defined by race/ethnicity and language ministries. Why aren't more local churches able to create and maintain intercultural ministry?

Within the Epistles is contained the blueprint for inter-cultural/interracial ministry: "There is neither Jew nor Gentile, neither slave nor free, nor is there male and female, for you are all one in Christ Jesus" (Galatians 3:28, NIV). In the body of Christ, the dividing lines of race, ethnicity, class, and gender fall away and we are made one. This is not to say that the particularities of our differences fade away. In fact, 1 Corinthians 12 details the important role diversity plays in providing wholeness within the body of Christ. Differences are required if the body is to thrive.

Is the church's inability or unwillingness to embrace the diversity found within and beyond its walls a reason for our decline in the twenty-first century? In an era when other institutions recognize diversity's importance in enhancing community, for the church to remain monocultural relegates us to the status of a quaint antique.

The Disturbance of Diversity

Perhaps we have made church too safe, too nice, too sanitized. Diversity does make things messier. It requires us to get out of our comfort zones, confront our own biases, and roll up our sleeves to do the hard work of building beloved community. It necessitates a new way of thinking of self and community. It moves the focus of my thinking from inward to outward, connecting with the expressions of truth found in lives that look much different from my own. It causes my carefully constructed worldview to be disturbed by the injustices done to others, and it requires a response. Yet, when we dare to live together, listening deeply to one another, allowing ourselves to learn from one another, we finally discover that we are creating and journeying toward beloved community.

"Hear my humble cry!" The hymn writer was directing this plea to Jesus Christ, but today, I believe the cries are to those within the church, its pews, and pulpits. The poor, dispossessed, and oppressed are crying for justice. As long as their voices and stories are not integrated into our community, as long as some topics are off limits or considered a mission moment which does not require any real commitment or change from individuals or the institution, the church fails to help a broken world find wholeness. It cannot with any credibility critique injustice. It ceases to be a witness to the world of the glorious diversity that is found within God's beloved creation.

"Do not pass me by!"

Notes

1. Fanny J. Crosby, "Pass Me Not, O Gentle Savior," AlltheLyrics.com, accessed January 18, 2016, http://www.allthelyrics.com/lyrics/douglas_miller/pass_me_not -lyrics-1268544.html.

2. Julian C. McPheeters, *The Life Story of Lizzie H. Glide* (San Francisco: Eagle Printing Company, 1936), 27.

3. Lewis E. Durham, *Glide Foundation from 1962–1967* (San Francisco: Glide Paper, 1967), 4.

4. From the memoirs of Rev. John Moore, pastor of Glide, October 1, 1962 to June 30, 1966. Undated document, Glide archives.

5. Gerald Adams, "Glide Memorial's Special Karma," *California Living*, April 25, 1971, 14.

6. Adams, "Glide Memorial's Special Karma," 14.

7. Cecil Williams and Janice Mirikitani, *Beyond the Possible: 50 Years of Creating Radical Change at a Community Called Glide* (New York: HarperOne, 2013), 128.

8. Williams and Mirikitani, *Beyond the Possible*, 132.

9. Williams and Mirikitani, *Beyond the Possible*, 132–33.

10. Williams and Mirikitani, *Beyond the Possible*, 137–38.

11. Pew Research Center, Religion and Public Life, "Members of the United Methodist Church," accessed March 20, 2016, http://www.pewforum.org/religious-landscape-study/religious-denomination/united-methodist-church/.

12. Accessed February 20, 2016, http://s3.amazonaws.com/Website_GCFA/Data_Services/Lay_2014_-_EthMemGen.xls.

13. Ibid.

CHAPTER 12

New Wineskins

Rev. Peter Ahn

Metro Community Church is a twelve-year-old church plant in northern New Jersey, an area less than five miles from Manhattan made up of predominantly wealthy suburbs. Upon graduation from seminary in 2003, my wife and I, along with eleven other people, came together to birth our dream of an ethnically diverse church. There were a handful of intercultural churches in the New York metropolitan area at the time, but none in northern New Jersey.

Hoping to grow the church, I had been meeting with dozens of people from all different backgrounds. I shared with them the vision of Metro Community Church, specifically how I felt God had called us to be an intercultural church. The majority of the meetings usually ended with the other person telling me that it didn't seem like the right fit for him or that she loved the vision but didn't think it could be done. Out of concern for me, these individuals often relayed cautionary tales of churches that had tried to accomplish this multiethnic dream and had tragically failed.

Needless to say, I was sorely disappointed. It became very clear, at that point, that the process of birthing and nurturing a church like Metro would be an intensely difficult and a laborious one. However, twelve years later, our weekly attendance ranges from 750 to 800 people. We are 65 percent Asian, 15 percent black (African American, Jamaican, and African), 10 percent Hispanic, and 10 percent white. The median age of our congregation falls somewhere between late twenties and early thirties.

How did we do it? What did we do differently to get to this point in our journey? I believe it's all in our ministry philosophy, which I'll call the New Wineskins.

Metro's Ministry Philosophy

The past twelve years have unquestionably been both the most challenging, as well as richest, years of my life, largely in part because of our church's unique ministry philosophy. Living out our church's philosophy continues to be painstakingly difficult for me, as well as for the people of our church. This is because Metro's ministry philosophy is so fundamentally countercultural to our society and counterintuitive to our humanity. So what, then, is Metro's ministry philosophy? It is simply *to find our commonality in our weaknesses, not our strengths*.

This is what New Wineskins ministry is all about: ministering out of our weakness so that God's strength can be perfected in us. It is complete acknowledgment that God's redemptive hand works at its maximum capacity in our weaknesses. Jesus spoke to John's disciples about new wineskins (Matthew 9:14-17).

New wine cannot be stored in old wineskins, as its effervescence will stretch the shriveled and hard old wineskins, ultimately causing them to burst. New wineskins are needed for new wine. Jesus' message in this passage is that Old Testament regulations regarding ceremonial defilement cannot stand before the joy of forgiveness, fellowship, excitement, and new direction that the coming of the kindom inaugurates. We, as Christians, cannot continue to minister in the old wineskins, showcasing only the strengths in the highlight reels of our lives. We must fully embrace the new wineskins by ministering honestly out of our weaknesses and brokenness.

At the pastoral level, ministry birthed from weakness requires a tremendous degree of transparency. This translates into deeply honest and personal Sunday sermons that allow the church to look into my own life. The people of Metro must be able to see, hear, and relate to my weaknesses, both past and present, so that they also may find hope as they struggle through life with Jesus Christ.

Christ's words to Paul, as recorded in 2 Corinthians 12:9 (NIV), provide a foundation for this ministry: "My grace is sufficient for you, for my power is made perfect in weakness." In understanding this verse, we must acknowledge that God's grace is most powerfully at work in our lives when we are weak. The Bible presents a theological synthesis that demonstrates how God's grace is most powerfully at work in our weakness.

Why do you think God waited until Abraham was one hundred years old and Sarah was in her nineties before they welcomed their promised child, Isaac? Why did God choose Moses to lead his people out of Egypt when Moses was a fugitive in his eighties with a speech impediment? Why did God choose a thirteen-year-old to give birth to the Messiah? The answer to these questions is one and the same. God's grace is most powerfully at work in human weakness.

If Christians truly desire God's grace to be most powerfully at work in our lives, it is crucial that we recognize that God will work, not through our strengths, but through our weaknesses. At Metro Community Church, we choose to be transparent, intentionally placing ourselves in a state of weakness and vulnerability, believing that, in our weakness, God's power is perfected. As our church congregation lives out our ministry philosophy, it is our responsibility to be open about sharing our hurts, struggles, sins, and brokenness with one another. It is essential that I lead by example by allowing myself to be vulnerable and transparent when I preach on Sundays. This provides the congregation the opportunity to see me just as I am, not as some super-spiritual giant but as someone who is flawed, hurting, and troubled, just like they are. But the story does not end there. In Christ, there is always redemption. After sharing my weaknesses and vulnerabilities with the congregation, I always follow up by sharing the redemptive aspect of my story.

The heart of the gospel is the redemption we experience through the grace of God. Nevertheless, the beauty of redemption can be fully appreciated and understood only when we are able to experience the actual depths from which we have been redeemed. Pastors and church leaders are often guilty of glossing over this essential step. To illustrate this point further, let's take a look at Easter.

Easter is one of the most celebrated occasions in any church. But the celebration of Easter is beautiful only because we experience it through the lens of Good Friday. Without Jesus' death on the cross, Easter would lose its power. Yes, those who believe in Jesus Christ would still be reconciled to God. But the beauty and wonder of Easter is derived from the agony and ugliness of the cross. Jesus' resurrection is all the more powerful because we know what happened three days prior. It is puzzling to me that pastors and church leaders continue to proclaim God's redemption in their lives while completely disregarding the Good Friday moments in their own experiences. Unfortunately, this is a hollow gospel. When we minister exclusively out of our strengths, thereby excluding the challenges that we often face as Christ followers, we diminish the redemptive power of the gospel.

Young people today are jaded by the church's inability to connect their lives with Jesus Christ. The church has adopted the mainstream culture's way of finding our commonality in our strengths. People outside the church will never identify with our Christian strengths. If you wake up at six in the morning and read the Bible, that is a wonderful strength. Nevertheless, the world will not identify with it. But if you wake up at six in the morning to read the Bible as a way to cope with the depression you have developed from growing up in an abusive home, then people both outside and inside of the church will be able to identify with you.

Pain shows no discrimination. Regardless of our ethnic background, gender, age, or socioeconomic class, pain finds all of us. For this reason, if we are truly to be a diverse church in which people from all races, socioeconomic classes, and generations can gather together, the church and its leaders absolutely must find their commonality in their weaknesses and not their strengths.

Most churches in the United States are ethno-specific.[1] As a result, the church has become the greatest institution in the nation that perpetuates ethnic segregation, both intentionally and unintentionally. This is because we view our ethnicity as a strength and a common source of pride. However, unless the church is willing to find its commonality in their congregants' weaknesses and not their strengths, it will, more often than not, be divided ethnically.

I still remember vividly the first time I shared my story in the pulpit. My palms were sweaty; my stomach was in knots; nervousness permeated every fiber of my being. I had doubts and fears about sharing my childhood story. But as I was standing on the stage looking at the people, I knew that as difficult as this was going to be, I needed to be the example of Metro's ministry philosophy—the new wineskins. This is what I shared that day:

> My family and I immigrated to the U.S. when I was three months old. My parents came to America because I was a sick child, and South Korea at the time was a developing nation with limited medical resources. The doctors encouraged my parents to immigrate to America if they wanted to ensure the safety of my life. My parents had lost a son due to health issues several years previously, and the pain of possibly losing another, their only son, was all the motivation they needed to move to the U.S.
>
> My father was from North Korea and fought in the Korean War. He came from a broken family. His mother had passed away at a young age, not long after his birth. He lived with a stepmother who physically, emotionally, and verbally abused him. When my father was able to muster enough courage to tell his dad what his wife had done to him, he was hopeful that his dad would listen and respond accordingly. However,

his hopes were dashed to pieces when his dad physically beat him and blamed him for tattle telling. My grandfather would consistently take the side of his wife, rather than believe his son. It was a harsh upbringing for my father—never experiencing any love from his father and stepmother.

My father defected from North Korea to South Korea during the Korean War. Eventually he met my mother and married her. The lack of love that my father had experienced as a child made it almost impossible for him to be a good husband and father. He was a hurting and lonely man. He would often come home after work, drunk and ready to take out his frustrations and pain on my mother, my sisters, and me. Needless to say, those years were very painful as I saw my father beat my mother— sometimes to a pulp—and was the recipient of that physical abuse myself when beating my mother was not enough for him. From a young age, I experienced my father as my primal foe. The venom of hate toward him was so strong that I often told myself that, when I got older, I would gladly repay him for all the pain he inflicted on us. His punishment would fit his crime, and I would be sure to be the one administering it.

One weekend, while I was home from college, my sister shared with me for the first time some stories of the abuse she had received from my father. Upon hearing her speak, I felt that the day of retribution had finally come. I was more than ready to take matters into my own hands. I proceeded down the stairs to where my father was sleeping, and I grabbed a knife in the kitchen. When I was eight steps away from taking his life, I asked how God could give us a father who didn't protect and love us. Why did God have to give my family a man who had destroyed each of us? It was one of the most broken and weak points in my entire life. Ironically, however, that was the pivotal moment in which God met me. My meeting with God that day jumpstarted a journey toward forgiveness and redemption that ultimately led me to forgive my father and begin rebuilding our marred relationship.

I remember being quite emotional as I shared this story. When I looked up and saw our church congregation, I noticed that many were crying and wiping tears. After the service was over, people came up to me and shared with me how they were impacted by my story. The common thread in their response was that they had experienced the gospel message through it. Our congregation connected with the honest sharing of my weaknesses, and this in turn empowered them to want to live more passionately for Jesus.

Empowering people to follow Jesus is exponentially more effective than guilt-tripping people. For the past twelve years, I have been consistently sharing the Good Friday moments of my life before sharing the Easter moments. What never fails to amaze me is that, regardless of what type of setting or church I am in, people who connect through weakness are always empowered with a genuine desire to want to be more faithful to God. This is the beauty and power of connecting through our weakness and vulnerability. People from across all different cultures, generations, and socioeconomic classes can relate to my stories because pain and struggle are part of the universal human experience.

Challenges Along the Way

While it's wonderful to be able to celebrate the wins, I would be remiss to leave out the bumps and hurdles we've faced along the way at Metro. If I practice transparency about our congregational life, I must disclose that we have had our fair share of growing pains during this twelve-year journey. As a result, we've learned the importance of always remaining alert to new opportunities for insight and clarity on how we can live out our ministry philosophy of embracing our weakness.

What we did not foresee was how difficult it would be for our people to identify with brokenness of a broader nature, more specifically, that which pertains to racial discrimination. For instance, I realized that identification with the personal experience of another—such as an abusive childhood or a struggle with addiction—comes naturally to people because this type of brokenness transcends ethnic and cultural lines and appeals to the universal human experience. However, I have found that it is infinitely more difficult for a person to relate to brokenness of a more culturally or racially specific nature, such as discrimination or racism that exists on a macro level (societally) but is experienced by only a minority group.

For example, it would be a challenge for our Latin American community to understand fully the layers of historical tension and brokenness that have existed between the Koreans and Japanese. The Japanese government occupied the Korean peninsula from the late 1800s to the mid-1900s, and the Korean people experienced such brutal and dehumanizing oppression under Japan's rule that these atrocities continue to cause hostility and division between the Japanese and Koreans today. These aftereffects continue to reverberate decades later, and sometimes even create strain between Japanese American and Korean American communities in the United States. Brokenness of this nature would be difficult for our Latin American community to grasp because it is so culturally specific to the Korean and Japanese communities.

One such learning moment for our church, through which I discovered just how difficult it truly is to identify with brokenness of a broader nature, occurred during the Trayvon Martin tragedy. Our church failed to provide a forum for our black brothers and sisters to grieve the brokenness they experienced when they watched another black life being taken merely for the pigmentation of his skin. Our church failed to address this in any capacity, and as a result, some of our black congregation members had to resort to attending other local black churches in town in order to grieve.

To be perfectly honest, the fault was mine. I was so caught up in the busyness of ministry and life that the thought of pausing and reflecting on how the Trayvon Martin tragedy would affect our black brothers and sisters at Metro did not even occur to me. I couldn't identify with the African American narrative because it was so different from my own narrative—the Asian American narrative.

Ultimately, this learning moment led to a meeting between our church leaders and the black congregation members of our church. We apologized for our error and asked these brothers and sisters to teach us how to better come alongside them in the context of the racial disparities they feel in this nation. Since then, we have actively participated in prayer vigils surrounding the Black Lives Matter movement. We have protested on the streets of Englewood, standing side by side with our black brothers and sisters, in order to show support and solidarity. We are also excited to launch a task force this year that will offer stronger leadership on how our church can have more integrity in matters of racial reconciliation.

Another struggle that our church has faced in its journey toward cultural diversity is related to the worship music that we sing on Sundays. I have had numerous conversations and confrontations with our previous worship directors on the importance of diversifying the music we sing on Sundays. Some have fought me, through and through, asserting that worship is more about the heart of worship than the style of worship, and while I agree with that statement to a great extent, I also believe that to shy away from diversifying the worship music we sing would be to overlook the racism that is being perpetuated in the church.

Now, you may be asking, "How does worship music perpetuate racism?" The sad truth is that racism is blatant in the Christian music industry. White evangelicals currently dominate the Christian music industry through Christian Contemporary Music (CCM), and the majority of artists who make up this genre are white.[2] While very few Christians will admit this, the CCM industry has perpetuated racial segregation with enormous success. Today, the chances of a black, Latino, or Asian artist succeeding in the CCM industry are slim to none.

I have challenged our worship directors to diversify the worship music we sing on Sundays, lest we continue to uphold this brokenness in our church. If the church is a place where we gain a foretaste of heaven, then it is only right that its music also be a representation of the citizens who will be in heaven: "and there before me was a great multitude that no one could count, from every nation, tribe, people and language, standing before the throne and before the Lamb" (Revelation 7:9, NIV).

A church that is permeated with new wineskins will become increasingly passionate, sensitive, and proactive about issues pertaining to racism, sexism, classism, and social justice. This is because these very issues are rooted in weakness. Providing a platform for our congregation members to become aware of their own weaknesses naturally leads them to an increased awareness of the social inequities of our society.

The Future of the Church Becoming Intercultural

It is a sad but indisputable fact that today's church has adopted a consumerist culture in which people come to maximize their own benefit.[3] Many visitors at Metro will share with me that they are looking for a church where they can be fed. I encourage them to view church, not through the lens of what they can get out of it, but rather, as a sacred place where they can worship God and serve to advance the kin-dom through their brokenness. Our philosophy of finding our commonality in our weakness is not one for the consumerist churchgoer. This philosophy bids us to embrace our brokenness, the brokenness of other people, and the brokenness in the world.

There is little hope for a church to grow as an intercultural congregation if it does not intentionally embrace and live out this identity as a new wineskin. Without it, the church is fated to continue as the ethno-specific church it is now. If church pastors and leaders do not adopt this new wineskin, their churches will continue to remain irrelevant to people inside and outside their walls. This is why it is absolutely critical for pastors and church leaders to lead out of their brokenness. As I stated earlier, pain shows no discrimination. It finds us all, at one point or another, regardless of where we live, how we speak, or what we look like. I strongly encourage leaders of the church to tap into their own brokenness and show people how their mourning can be turned into dancing.

I love the fact that I can relate and connect with Jesus' brokenness as depicted in the Gospels. The truth is, none of us can relate to Jesus' strength. Paul reminded us in Romans 3:23 that we have all sinned and fallen short of God's glory. However, we can all relate to Jesus' brokenness, weakness, and humanity. I love the story of Jesus at the Garden of Gethsemane, confessing to his three closest disciples that his soul was overwhelmed to the point of death (Matthew 26:36-46). This honest glimpse into Jesus' humanity is so encouraging to me, as I have also experienced such moments in my life when I felt that the pain was too much for me to bear and wondered if death would be preferable.

Another of my favorite scenes from Jesus' life was when he wept with Mary and Martha over the death of Lazarus, even though he had every intention of raising Lazarus from the dead just moments later (John 11:33). As a pastor, I have had many opportunities to share in the grief of those in my congregation over the loss of friends and family members.

On one occasion, I received an urgent phone call from the family member asking me to rush to the hospital because his eight-month-old baby had been killed. The child's mother had been in the middle of her daily walk with her baby, when a careless bus driver drove into a metal pole. The pole landed on the baby's head, and the infant died. The hours after I received that phone call were easily the worst hours of my entire career as pastor. When I entered the hospital and met with the parents, all I could do was weep with them, the way Jesus had wept with Mary and Martha. I didn't offer them a theological answer as to why this had happened, but instead, I provided a shoulder for them to cry on. We wept together in that hospital room because, in those moments of pain and agony, an embrace of solidarity was infinitely more powerful than any answer I could have given. Jesus taught me the importance of weeping with those who are weeping.

Another moment of Jesus' life that allows me to connect with him through weakness is his crucifixion. Jesus was hanging on the cross in agony and pain and didn't respond the way a superhero would. Instead, Jesus responded in a way that is probably familiar to any one of us who has undergone hardships that seemed unbearable. Jesus cried out, "My God, my God, why have you forsaken me?" (Mark 15:34, NIV).

There have been countless low points in my life, especially in relation to my father, when I truly felt that God had forsaken me. But a powerful thing happens in our lives when we find we can relate to Jesus' brokenness. We realize that Jesus understands our brokenness because he was broken too. We don't worship a distant God who sits up in heaven and listens to our cries, only to be unable to truly relate or empathize with what we are going through. Our God understands us and weeps with us because God, also, was broken many times—literally and figuratively—when the Word became flesh and entered human history two thousand years ago.

Embracing and finding our commonality in our weaknesses is the new wineskin that Metro has been living out for the past twelve years. This philosophy not only allows us to be a community in which we can build bridges for deeper racial reconciliation, it also strengthens us as Christ's disciples.

There is something unimaginably beautiful that happens when we experience God's presence in the midst of the darkest hours of our lives. When we are transparent about our pain with ourselves, God, and others, we experience an oasis of hope, love, forgiveness, understanding, and peace in the midst of our broken lives. This is the power that is perfected in our weakness that Paul described in 2 Corinthians 12:9.

The time has come for the church and its leaders to rise up and lead out of their brokenness. If leading out of our weakness affords us the opportunity to tap into God's perfect strength in order to relate and connect deeply with other people from other cultures and their brokenness, then how can we not be more willing and passionate about drinking from this new wineskin? What is holding you back from throwing away the old wineskin and drinking from the living water that this new wineskin has to offer?

My hope and prayer is that a new day will emerge for the church—a day in which its leaders can be honest about the challenges and struggles of leading out of our brokenness but can also rejoice in the joy, peace, love, and hope of God's redemptive work in us as we give God full authority over our weakest, most vulnerable moments. Embrace your brokenness, and may God's power be perfected in you!

Notes

1. Michael Lipka, "The Most and Least Racially Diverse U.S. Religious Groups," Pewresearch.org, accessed July 27, 2015, http://www.pewresearch.org/fact-tank/2015/07/27/the-most-and-least-racially-diverse-u-s-religious-groups.

2. John Daniel Lindenbaum, "The Industry, Geography, and Social Effects of Contemporary Christian Music," Gradworks.umi.com, accessed October 26, 2016, http://gradworks.umi.com/33/83/3383280.html.

3. Derwin L. Gray, "God Is Not Santa Claus," Christianitytoday.com, accessed November 20, 2014, http://www.christianitytoday.com/derwin-gray/2014/november/god-is-not-santa-claus.html.

CHAPTER 13

Long Thread, Lazy Girl

Rev. Katie Mulligan

When I was a girl, my mother became ill and was paralyzed for a time. Over several years she patiently taught her body how to move again. Sometimes in the quiet of that house, she embroidered. I sat beside her and watched the needle push through the cloth, front to back, back to front, a knot here, a knot there. Twisting, turning, flashing needle, the colorful thread, and a picture so slowly emerging on the blank canvas. Finish a small section, loosen the hoop, move the hoop, tighten it again, more flowers. Until one day, the threaded painting was finished, and stretched out there on the cloth was a large pot of hundreds of flowers, bursting with color and beauty. The canvas was three feet tall by two feet wide, and it took three years to fill it with flowers. As she stitched, she healed.

One day she began to teach me. She gave me a small, 8-inch-square canvas, a simple design, and a small plastic hoop. And then it was my needle pushing through the cloth, front to back, back to front, a knot here, a knot there. Fabric held tight by the hoop, but the thread—oh, the thread! Twisting and turning and tangling in the back, and tangled thread doesn't sit right, doesn't pull right, and doesn't look right. It was so tempting, always, to cut a long piece of thread—one starting knot, one ending knot, less cutting, less frustration. But, too long of a thread and it would tangle and twist and turn until the stitches became ugly and impossible, and there was nothing for it but to cut them out and start over. Wasting thread, wasting time, fraying the canvas.

My mother would smile and nod, "Long thread, lazy girl!" The lessons I learned profoundly shape my ministry work. When my work gets tangled, as intercultural ministry often does, I remember, "Long thread, lazy girl!"

I have carried this phrase with me all these years. As I think about intercultural ministry, this phrase is both cautionary and hopeful. Intercultural ministry (and the required introspection to accomplish it) is an intricate, careful work that takes many years. As we carefully thread the needle and tie the knots, we might embroider a spectacular painting and heal ourselves along the way.

(Re)locating Myself

I grew up in the suburbs of Santa Barbara, California, a white, middle-class girl. Many of my classmates were Hispanic, and a few were of Asian descent. As far as I can remember we had three black students in our school. I grew up navigating mostly white spaces as a white woman, without giving a second thought to the privilege that it entails. These days I am a divorced, queer, single mother, female pastor. That identity is a complicated mess to navigate inside the church, although few people outside the church care. It wasn't until seminary that I began to interrogate whiteness, either in myself or in the world.

In 2006, when I first arrived at seminary in New Jersey, I took a class on liberation theology. Although the books were instrumental in furthering my education about culture, class, race, gender, sexuality, and other intersections, it was the interaction with people that challenged me most. One day in our class, I had a conversation with a black woman I had not met before. After class she was talking with a friend of mine. I approached them, held out my hand, and said, "I'm Katie. Tell me your name." The woman looked at me with irritation and said, "What do you need to know my name for?" Uncertain, uncomfortable, awkward, I took a step back and put my hand down. "I guess I don't," I replied. It had never occurred to me that I wasn't entitled to know someone's name.

It took two years of seminary, many books, and several classes before I sorted through that one interaction. I came to understand that I held a sense of white entitlement in this world that extended to ownership over other people. I still squirm when I realize this about myself. I'm still learning. Every time I think maybe I've got a handle on whiteness, I find another place within, grasping at power and control. I get exasperated with myself. I keep going.

Long thread, lazy girl! I take slow, painstaking steps to discover who I am and how I move in this world. To do intercultural work, we must do the personal work. We must locate ourselves in the work, patiently. The world is constantly shifting; we ourselves are constantly shifting, and whiteness is slick and sly and deceptive.

Engaging Intercultural Ministry

These days I find myself moving in black spaces with black people. My work and life shifts toward Trenton, New Jersey, a little more each day. And with that shift comes the uncomfortable awareness of the culture of white supremacy and oppression I bring with me, even and especially through my work with the church.

I've been thinking a lot about intercultural ministry. The ministry I work with is at a critical crossroads, and I am not sure it will survive the decisions that have to be made. For the last four years I have worked with three churches together to create one collaborative youth group. Each of the churches, mostly suburban white congregations, has maintained its own culture and ways, but the youth groups combined to create one youth ministry, which we hoped would develop its own cohesive culture. One of our churches, located exactly on the border of the suburbs and the city, is experiencing demographic change faster than the other two churches. The neighborhood around that church is now a primarily black neighborhood. When I attended the eighth-grade graduation ceremony last year, every child who graduated was either black or Hispanic or both.

The church held a Thanksgiving dinner for the community, and a young black girl came with her family. She started to play with the white daughter of a church member, and their Sunday school teacher offered to bring her to church if she wanted to come again. The girl brought her cousin. And then they brought three friends. And suddenly the Sunday school and youth ministry was now suburban middle/working-class white and urban working-class/poor black.

The five youth brought five more and then five more, and we've been navigating what might be considered intercultural ministry ever since. I say "might be" because it has been four years, and I am unsure of how sustainable this ministry is, how much we have learned from one another, and whether it is good to continue in the way we have gone. I say "might be" because the invitation to write this chapter identified intercultural ministry as bringing people of various cultures together to engage in learning from one another, giving equal value and power to each culture.[1]

Critical Reflection

In reflecting upon this definition of intercultural ministry, I am not sure that this is something our ministry has accomplished over the last four years. The churches, our volunteer leaders, and our youth have decisions to make at this juncture.

When I think deeply about intercultural ministry, and about all of the intentionality, resources, time, and energy that would be required to claim what we are about as intercultural ministry, my mother's voice rings through, "Long thread, lazy girl!" All I can see is that it may be time to cut this thread and start a fresh knot.

I've come to think about this ministry when I read the Song of Songs. While some traditions view that biblical book as a romantic love poem with a happily ever after, that's not what I see in its words. Two lovers come together, unexpectedly, neither prepared for the relationship. They exclaim over one another, rejoicing in each other's beauty. Their love is a bubble, set apart from everyday reality, separate, private, and incomplete.

As we read along through the Song perhaps we remember our own unexpected, impossible, delightful love affairs. Perhaps we remember too that our initial passion is not always a match for the reality of culture, religion, class, race, gender, sexuality, social condemnation, family, money, children, illness, suffering, war. If our initial passion is to become relationship, a change/maturation /transformation is required. What began as delightful happenstance must continue with thoughtful intention and a careful navigation of power structures. Or it must end.

Long thread, lazy girl! It is so easy to get ahead of myself! It is easy to remember the finished tapestry of my mother's healing and forget the days and years of careful stitching. It is easy to think that because black and white children are standing in the same room that something has been accomplished—that the painting is done. Intercultural ministry requires more.

The youth group had a hopeful moment last summer, and I offer it up as a tiny thread, difficult to knot. Not perfection—we may have to undo this stitch yet. But I am hopeful.

The weekend retreat was going badly, and I had all but given up hope of accomplishing anything useful with our students. Most of our volunteers had canceled last minute, and many of our students chose not to come. Two adults (including me) and ten students showed up. The whole evening had gone poorly, and the students were in a rotten mood. Nothing I planned was holding their attention, and they were squabbling with one another as only siblings can. There were tensions between the five white students and five black students that everybody was afraid to name (and to be honest, I am still sometimes afraid to name and claim).

As we approached the 10:00 p.m. hour, I decided to try one last activity and then call it a night, trusting that Jesus would make something of this mess I'd created. The students and I gathered in the sanctuary and made a circle with the chairs, and then we tried out a few exercises from a book called *Games for Actors and Non-Actors* by Augusto Boal.[2] I had some ambitions to create a group focused on Boal's Theatre of the Oppressed, and these exercises were intended to be the beginning of forming that group.

The first exercise was to make a circle in the air with the right hand. After a minute, I asked the students to simultaneously make a cross in the air, using their left hands. The group began to relax into laughter as they realized the impossible task they'd been set.

A few minutes later I asked them to try something new: make a circle with their right foot, and then after a minute try to also write their name in the air with their right hand. There was more laughter and more moving toward frustration.

We grew bolder and moved on to the third exercise. The students joined with a partner. One of the pair was tasked with being the leader. The other half of the pair was to be the follower. The leader's job was to place their hand as close to their partner's face as possible and then slowly move their hand in different directions. The follower's job was to move their head according to their leader's hand movements, keeping their head as close to the leader's hand as possible. The pair was supposed to work up to more complex movements so that over a few minutes the follower's movements could become quite contorted as they followed the leader's hand.

The students dove in with gusto. Immediately they moved too fast with each other, leaders reveling in their sudden power to bend another person to their will. Frustrated comments started pouring out. I urged the students to slow down. More frustration. After a few minutes I told the students to switch places. The followers became the leaders; the leaders became the followers.

Retribution was swift and brutal. The new leaders immediately moved their hands into positions their partners could not possibly follow. One pair was slow to get started, and as I watched them begin, the leader shoved her hand straight toward her partner's face. The follower, startled and angry, yelled, "I'm done," punched her partner in the chest, and sat down with her arms folded.

I told everyone to sit down and take a deep breath. I thought for sure the exercise was a mistake. I asked the girl who punched her partner to share why she got violent, and she began to explain how she didn't like having someone's hands so close to her face. Her partner had scared her with the quick movement, and her body reacted. She was a little embarrassed and a lot angry. Her partner apologized.

As a group, we began to talk about bodies and movement and boundaries and touch. After a little while our conversation turned to race and how black youth faced higher levels of violence in their neighborhoods.

I told them the story of my first youth group meeting with this church. Two of the students at the retreat had been present for that first meeting in 2012. I had formed four groups of students, and there were two black students who were inseparable. In an effort to be "more diverse," I had assigned a white student, "Tamara," to their group. Or at least I thought she was white. Tamara began to give me a hard time about being racist: "You put all the black girls in one group, Katie!" Thinking she was being insensitive and difficult, I started to lecture her about race and racism and how this youth group wasn't going to perpetuate racism, when suddenly she burst into laughter. "I'm black, stupid!" she yelled, while still laughing.

Three years later, Tamara was still laughing hard at the memory, along with the other black students at the retreat. They were laughing at me and with me. I was laughing with them at my own earnest ignorance. I glanced over at the white students and realized none of them were laughing. They were frozen in fear.

We all stopped laughing about the same time, and the room got very quiet. The students suddenly realized that they had organized their chairs by race, with black students on one side of the circle and white students on the other. The white students couldn't speak. The black students didn't know what to say. One of them said quietly, "We're just laughing . . . It was funny . . ." and then it was quiet again.

One of the white students finally spoke through his fear and said, "It's just not funny to laugh about race. I don't want to be called a racist. It's just not funny." The room was too quiet and sad. And it became very awkward.

After a minute, one of the black students got up and sat next to one of his white friends. (And here is where the stitch needs work—how do we ever navigate the power piece when it always falls on those oppressed to make the first move toward reconciliation?) He didn't speak; he just moved to break the tension and comfort his friend. One of the white girls moved to sit next to one of her black friends. They rearranged themselves, almost defiantly, and stared at me. We looked around and realized: now they were seated by gender, with all the girls on one side and all the boys on the other.

The room burst into laughter as we realized the impossibility of it all. It is impossible to escape these intersections of race and gender and class and sexuality. For less than an hour we explored those intersections and the ways our bodies carry those distinctions. We argued and laughed and discussed, and the group drew tighter together in some small way that is hard to define or measure. It was . . . hopeful . . .

. . . and sad at the same time. It was a tiny thread, a tiny knot, in a much larger pattern to be threaded. I've reflected on that moment. Why were our white youth unable to break the tension first? What could or should I have done differently as the youth pastor? And I've reflected on how to follow up on that exercise. There have been precious few openings to continue that conversation. The churches and our volunteers have been reluctant to dig deep into this conversation. The youth have not reengaged. I have been hesitant.

Long thread, lazy girl! Perhaps it was just a moment. Perhaps I am too close to see what it might mean. It is so hard to claim this as intercultural ministry.

Tangled Threads

A love affair, we've been having—with all the delight of isolated passion, not having to think too hard about the future—who knows if the youth group has a future? Arise, my fair one! Come away with me! Come roller skating! Eat pizza! How beautiful you are, my love, how very beautiful! This is my new best friend! How much better is your love than wine! Yes! Let's go to camp—it will be beautiful and amazing and perfect!

The churches fell into this ministry without thinking about it. Some students asked to come, and the youth group opened the door and said yes. And I am so glad we did! Relationships formed across racial and class lines that would not have been possible without this strange youth ministry in-between. But there are tensions and cracks deepening, and I am unsure of the future. We may have cut the thread too long. Perhaps there should have been multiple threads. We might have to pull the stitches out and start again. The churches might have to put this project down and stop.

Song of Songs is not merely a passionate love poem with a happy ending. Risk and threat are woven through its chapters and verses. Foxes are ruining the vineyards and sentinels patrol the streets. The beloved is missing. There are alarms in the night. The sentinels turn violent toward the woman lover.

We experience similar dangers in the love story that is our youth ministry. Our volunteer leaders have struggled in our ministry to hold the tensions with honesty and justice. We have failed often.

Intercultural ministry as a model is daunting because it requires those with power to relinquish it. It requires those with power to acknowledge that they have it. It requires those with power to look at what we do not wish to see: ourselves.

As defined by this book's thesis, intercultural ministry gives equal value and power to each culture. In the segregated and oppressive space we are navigating, justice may require more than the promise of intercultural ministry. As our black students navigate primarily white churches, it is clear that the church members hold a great deal of power: money, white privilege, access to resources, voting power in the congregation, formal coded language, property (and access to space), familial ties to the church (and therefore strong advocacy for one's needs). Our black students lack this kind of power. They do not have much money; they are black moving in a white space; they cannot vote without membership; they cannot receive membership without the vote of those in power; they cannot access or manage the property; their families are not connected here. Their language, their noise level, their movements are differently cultured, and in the desperately quiet, still space of a Presbyterian church space, our black youth stand out starkly.

Without considerable work on the part of our three congregations, intercultural ministry will not be possible. It requires that our churches and members relinquish power, which as white, middle-class adults, we do not often acknowledge we possess. It has been a sudden love affair. Whether our work together as adults and youth matures into a long-term relationship remains to be seen, and we will have to navigate the power differentials.

A year ago, the church in the transitional neighborhood pulled out of the youth partnership. Many of their white families had transferred to other churches, and the church had not developed strong relationships with the black youth and their families. At the same time, the church experienced a change in pastoral leadership, dwindling financial resources, and a significant loss in membership.

The youth were louder, messier, more rambunctious, and less con-siderate of the older, quieter, more mature membership. Adding in the class, racial, and cultural differences, the youth group became more than the church was able or willing to resource and support. The remaining students connected to that church were black youth experiencing generational poverty and systemic racism. The most-ly white, wealthier, and older church members chose to disengage with the youth. My contract was not renewed, and the youth group was no longer able to meet in that church.

But it turns out that the claiming and naming of a space is not as straightforward as property ownership, and that power refuses to be confined in its "proper" places. The youth had been gone from this building for months, attending other church services, running our programs out of other spaces. One night an interfaith organi-zation held a prayer vigil back in our old building, and a few of our black students wanted to attend.

I picked them up and promised them dinner. The interfaith group would be praying that night for a young black boy who had been shot and killed in the neighborhood. There were other vigils, other services, other ways to grieve, but this night my students came with me. We went into this church, where we hadn't been for a year, in order to name his name and claim this space for their friend.

As the youth and I walked into the church building, one of the girls looked about the familiar hallway. She smiled, raised her hand high, and said, "We back, bitches!"

I wish that the congregation had been there to witness that moment, to see this girl reclaim the church as her own space. I wish that the church members and the youth were in a place of conver-sation where the congregation might understand this act as a young girl coming into her own God-given power. I wish that the church could claim her in the way she had just claimed the church. I wish that the church might match her level of fierce passion with a passion of its own that says, "This is hard, but we won't give up."

I think, in order for our youth group and churches to claim intercultural ministry, we will have to grapple with this girl's claim: "We back, bitches!" We will have to understand all of the layers of complexity to her seemingly simple pronouncement, including the implicit cry of injustice at having to be back in the first place. To claim intercultural ministry, the church would have to acknowledge her equal claim to this building, to membership, to the resources of the church, to God. We would have to seek after the source of our discomfort at her statement—at the language used, at the claim of ownership, at the strength of a young black girl refusing to be shut out.

Snipping the Thread, Tying the Knot

Long thread, lazy girl! Where shall we even start with our threaded needle? How long will this canvas take to fill? How impatient I am, have always been. How tangled my own work has always been.

"We back, bitches!" And I want it to be true! I want the youth group's moment of insight from last summer to mean more than it does. I want love and passion to be enough. I want to forget the sentinels and the foxes and the threats outside the bubble of our hopes and dreams. I want the hopes and dreams to be enough. But they are not. We are at the end of the Song, and I cannot tell you how it ends. I only know that there must be a shift. The churches will end the relationship. Or we will mature and grow and change so that something truer is possible.

I believe intercultural ministry may be possible—I even think it could be possible in the ministry in which I am now located. I also believe it will be a decades-long work to accomplish such a thing. At this crossroads the churches are considering several options for the future of this ministry. I have hopes that as a collaboration we will move forward in some fashion. If we do not, we will be left behind to choke on our own entitlement. The future of this world lies in intercultural work; more and more our children are insisting on it. The question for the church is whether we will move forward through our deep discomfort, relinquish power and control and resources, and allow ourselves to be deeply moved and changed by the claim cried out by a young girl, "We back, bitches!"

If you are asking me the next steps, I would say these things:

1. Long thread, lazy ministry! Move carefully and slowly. Pull out the stitches and start over when needed. Don't be afraid of slow progress. Take short threads. Do a little every day. Remember that this tapestry will take years to craft.

2. Interrogate yourselves often. Ask questions that make you squirm. Learn to recognize the grasping after power and control that will destroy relationship and community.

3. Recognize that equalizing power is not as simple as saying "We are all God's children." Some people hold greater power and demand greater value because of the intersections of race, class, money, religion, gender, sexuality, and so on. Some folks will be required to give up more than others.

4. Don't be afraid to stake a claim to your power over and against another's insistence. "We back, bitches!" might be the most important claim you can make when you have been pushed out.

5. Allow yourselves to heal.

6. Cherish the passion and delight and joy that come from unexpected lovers. However much you mature, transform, change, and do remember, "How beautiful you are!"

7. If you must end your intercultural love affair, may you never forget what has happened. May you speak of this time and this ministry over and again, hoping for what might be.

I sketch out pictures on my embroidery canvas sometimes, lightly, in pencil. Ultimately, whatever design I draw will be covered over by thousands of tiny knots and stitches. It is not really my painting to design and thread. What might it look like, though, this intercultural ministry? How might we move forward?

When I can, I attend a black church nested in one of our white churches. They pray for me and encourage me. They laugh heartily but gently at the image of me and my white self knocking on doors in the projects. They know, and I know, the history of whiteness in this city, what it has done to black folks, how it exploits and takes and leaves behind. The first time I came to worship with them, I stepped into the chapel as they were beginning to sing with recorded music, playing strong out of the speakers. I smiled with relief as I entered the space. The usher looked at me and said, "I'm sorry, is the music too loud? I'll turn it down." My astonishment matched hers as I asked for a bulletin and said I was here to worship with them.

As I reread this chapter I am convicted that this youth ministry is not intercultural, simply by the fact that it is white people and white churches deciding whether or not to continue the ministry. The black students have already spoken. They text every other day, "Miss Katie, you picking us up today?" They will have their ministry no matter what we do. But if we desire mutuality and equality, white folks gonna have to give up a lot: money, power, control, privilege, language. This relationship can't be about occupying the same space; intercultural ministry must be about fully inhabiting that space and resources. We'll have to turn up the microphones and the music, dance a little, live a little, love a lot more.

I have a picture in my mind of my black student standing in the pulpit and saying straight into the turned-up mic, "We back, bitches!" And the white Presbyterians picking up their bulletins and saying, "Thanks be to God!"

Notes

1. In their invitation to write this chapter, Kim and Aldredge-Clanton included this definition of intercultural ministry. This definition is also included in the introduction (p.xi.) to this book.

2. Augusto Boal, *Games for Actors and Non-Actors*, trans. Adrian Jackson, 2nd ed. (London: Routledge, 2005).

CHAPTER 14

Intercultural Ministry on a University Campus

Rev. David Hershey

The number of non-white students at my high school in rural Lancaster County in Pennsylvania could probably be counted on two hands. The church I grew up in, the Evangelical Congregational Church,[1] which is an offshoot of the Methodists, was filled with white people who faithfully sang hymns Sunday morning and, at least the elderly ones, attended prayer meeting Sunday night.

As I grew up I discovered that the majority of Christians were not old white people. But it was not until I went to college that I began to encounter the wider world in general and of Christianity in particular. I got involved in Christian Student Fellowship (CSF) at Penn State University, one of many evangelical ministries on campus. For the first time in my life I was part of a large group of people my own age who had a passion for Jesus.

Among the many new experiences I had with CSF were my first cross-cultural mission trips. Over spring break we went to North Carolina to help with recovery efforts after a hurricane. That Sunday we visited the church hosting us, and the CSF students were the only white faces in the congregation. The worship experience was new and memorable for me, from the vibrant and energetic gospel music to the sweaty preacher bringing God's Word in a powerful way I had never heard before. A few months later I joined a group of college students on a week-long trip to the Dominican Republic. My view of the world was changed as, for the first time, I met people who lived in houses with dirt floors or only three walls. It brought perspective to the life of privilege I lived back home.

The leader of our team was a Dominican named Henry. He was with us the whole week, sharing insights both about Dominican culture and the gospel. He instructed us on what to say as we went door to door and did evangelism. Henry led us as we put on two outreach events. When Henry asked if someone wanted to offer the Sunday sermon at the church hosting us, I volunteered before I even knew what I was saying.

This was the first time I ever preached, and it was with a translator. I do not remember what I said, but I must have said something good, for a number of people in the church began having an experience, verbally thanking God. This was also something new. When I was growing up, our church followed a formal order of worship and people expected to be home in time for lunch. Here the preacher stopped so that the Spirit could move.

My experiences at university shaped and changed me in big and small ways. I was so affected by campus ministry that for more than a decade now I have served on staff with CSF as campus minister at Penn State Berks.

Survey of Campus Ministry

This chapter will share a few reflections of what intercultural ministry on campus can look like. These reflections come from my experiences of both success and failure in trying to create a ministry that allows all sorts of people to have a voice. But first, I will give a brief background on campus ministry to set up the context.

History and Roots of Challenge
Many of the first universities founded in the United States had strong ties to specific Christian denominations and included spiritual formation as an essential component of campus life. Over time

these ties loosened, and by the 1900s the old private universities as well as the state schools had become secular in nature.[2] Outside organizations formed to fill in the gap and provide spiritual formation resources for those who desired it. Many of the major campus ministry organizations trace their beginnings to this time period.[3]

Developing in the early to mid-twentieth century, these evangelical groups were informed by North American evangelicalism and fundamentalism. The motivating factor for these organizations was to seek conversions on campus. The university was seen as a mission field.

The culture shaping these campus organizations, growing out of American evangelicalism, tended to be white and European and to speak a language understandable to other white and European persons. Thus the challenge has become how to continue work on campus among students of other ethnic backgrounds.

Illustrating the Challenge

A few summers ago I drove to Philadelphia to worship at the home church of one of my students. Nick is African American, and my wife and I were the only white faces at his Baptist church that morning. The service was filled with gospel music, interactive prayer, and passionate preaching. A few weeks later we again drove to Philadelphia, this time to Chinatown to worship at Bridget's Chinese church. We attended the English language service, which consisted of a praise band leading a few contemporary worship songs followed by a sermon focused on practical application.

While Nick's black Baptist church was quite different from what I am used to, Bridget's Chinese church in the city had a worship service that looked and felt much like contemporary worship services in white evangelical churches I was familiar with. I share these experiences simply to state one thing: when working toward intercultural ministry, there is no simple process. Every ethnic background is different; so too is every individual from each of those backgrounds. Intercultural ministry requires investing in learning from others, which begins with a lot of listening.

When we want to build an intercultural community on campus, one of the biggest challenges is the very nature of university life. College students are already stressed, busy, and in transition. They have to deal with exams, projects, and finding internships. Beyond that they have financial issues and personal relationships to deal with. Just getting them to care about and nurture their spiritual development while in college is a huge step. The further challenge is to take such spiritual development out of the realm of "what's in it for me."

If a student just wants to check off weekly attendance on a mental to-do list, that student may not be much interested in creating a racially diverse group. Creating intercultural ministries requires students who care for more than just their own private spiritual development, important as that may be.

In preparing this chapter I talked to friends who work in campus ministry, and they all saw intercultural ministry as important but difficult to create. The biggest challenge is that students tend to group with people like themselves. On campuses as in the rest of society, white kids tend to have mostly white friends, and black kids have mostly black friends. Campus ministries can work toward overcoming this challenge by emphasizing our common faith in Christ.

When students of different cultures have come together, the results are positive. Cady Wurtz, who ministers at Penn State, mentioned the benefits in the lives of students: "It definitely broadens their minds and lets them see what it would be like in other cultures."[4] She went on to speak about how these relationships have helped the students to be able to think more openly about others as they begin to see things from a different perspective. In an effort to promote such learning, a few of the ministers I spoke to mentioned mission trips. Nick Garrety, a graduate of Penn State who now ministers there, noted that students gain lasting experience from being "immersed in a culture outside their comfort zone" on such trips.[5]

Perhaps ironically, it may take getting students *off* campus for them to be confronted with a bit of diversity, opening their eyes to the possibilities of intercultural communities *on* campus. When students begin to get out of their comfort zones and learn from others, the benefits are obvious. Tim Diehl spent more than a decade with Intervarsity, and he told me, "When people engage cross-culturally they begin to understand the world, other people, themselves, even God, differently. . . . The art, literature, fashion, etc. of others now suddenly seems like a rich and welcome addition to a growing patchwork of beautiful diversity rather than a worrisome practice by some 'other.'"[6]

All humans are created in God's image and possess inherent worth and value. Further, Christians believe that the love of God in Jesus extends to people of "every nation, tribe, people and language" (Revelation 7:9, NIV). Thus, to be part of a Christian community that consists only of one ethnicity is to miss out on the full beauty of what God intends the church to be. The benefit for creating intercultural Christian communities on campus is that students begin to take part in the church as it was always meant to be.

Stories from PSU Berks

Penn State University consists of one huge main campus located in the middle of Pennsylvania, and more than a dozen satellite campuses sprinkled throughout the commonwealth. The Berks campus, located a one-hour drive from Philadelphia, is the home of about three thousand students, the majority of whom are white.[7] CSF at Penn State Berks is one of the longest-running student clubs on campus.

Each year CSF has a leadership team consisting of four or five core students who run the activities of the community. For five out of the last ten years, this team has had racial diversity. In my third year a student named Kevin, who was born in Kenya, served as president of the group. Following that, in my fourth year, our president was Nick, the African American student I mentioned above. Nick and I became quite close and I still keep in touch with him.

Nick was the sort of student you want in your ministry—a good-looking, easy-going extrovert who was involved in many clubs on campus. Everyone liked him. When he took on the leadership role, he was excited. I expected our numbers to double or triple solely due to his popularity and charisma. On nights we were meeting, Nick would walk around the dining hall inviting people to CSF.

Occasionally Nick would persuade some of his African American friends to come; there were even a few nights when we had more black students than white. But in general, our core group who attended each week remained mostly white, as it had been in years past. We were more diverse than we had been, but not as diverse as I thought we could be. I had breakfast with Nick and asked him if he thought some of his peers were wary of our community due to me. Was my style, my preaching, too white? He paused and mused that my whiteness might be a small part of it.

People tend to want to be with people like them. When white students pop their heads in the door and see a white guy leading, they automatically feel welcome. Black students may think twice about whether this community is for them.

When I was doing research for this chapter I emailed Nick, asking him a few questions. Mostly, how well did he think CSF did in reaching out to the diverse campus? Here was his response:

> I would highly agree the church should be populated by multiple cultures and leaders should strive to build an environment of variety of thought and culture. Fear comes from lack of knowledge. By bringing people, culture, and experience together, many barriers can be broken! Looking back on my experience with CSF I would say we were always "present."

We were always there on campus and open and accepting of new membership regardless of race.[8]

Nick clearly has positive memories of his time at PSU Berks, remembering CSF to be welcoming while also recognizing there are constant barriers to overcome. As Nick says, barriers can be broken if the hard work of creating a comfortable place where students can honestly share is undertaken.

It is also important to remember that while culture and ethnicity are a huge part of us, they are not our sole defining factors. White people may look at me and feel an automatic welcome. At the same time, not all white students who get involved in the ministry become friends with me. Some of them get to know me and do not like my style of teaching or leading. Some students connect with me around interests, theology, and much more. Nick and I had enough in common to overcome racial-cultural differences and work together to create a strong and diverse community in his time here.

It is equally important to remember when doing ministry across cultures that no single program or strategy will reach all white students or all black students or all Asian American students because, for all they do have in common related to race, no ethnic group is monolithic in its culture. For example, black students will encompass African Americans from various socioeconomic and regional backgrounds, as well as Africans, Haitians, black Hispanics, and more. Latino students may have the Spanish language in common, but they will represent multiple countries from Latin and South Americas, the Caribbean, and Spain. Their language fluency will add further diversity, particularly since some will be first-, second-, or even third-generation. Asian American students may have even less in common culturally, representing numerous nations, languages, and religious backgrounds. And those from Southeast Asia will have ethnic identities quite distinct from Asian countries such as Japan, North or South Korea, and China.

Consider another African American student with whom I have enjoyed working at Penn State Berks. Brianna has been a member of CSF for four years. I was interested to see what she would say about how well CSF welcomes people of different cultures. Brianna responded positively, similar to Nick: "I think that CSF did well in welcoming other cultures. Everyone wanted to talk to others and I don't think people saw that I was black but saw that I was a Christian person wanting to get closer to God just like they want to. . . . I don't think we see each other based on race, just that we are children of God."[9] In Brianna's experience, CSF has created a space for all people of any background to pursue their relationship with God and make new friends.

Some of the black students who have been a part of CSF were not like Nick and Brianna, born and raised in United States, but instead were more like Kevin, with memories of growing up in Africa. Recently we have had students from Ghana: a young man named Faith and another young man named Jude.

Both Jude and Faith speak of their faith in terms that sound very charismatic and Pentecostal. Faith has often shared the story of how he came to know Jesus, a story consisting of visions and supernatural experiences. Jude also has shared charismatic experiences. Theologically they have more in common with white Pentecostals than with the black Baptist church Nick grew up in. Sometimes such stories make me, with my more stoic rational faith, a bit uncomfortable. But people like me need to hear such stories, in order to create the communities we want to create.

I recently spoke with another African America student named Jewel, who is from Philadelphia and attends a church which she describes as Apostolic and fits into the charismatic tradition of worship. She surprised me by saying that one of the biggest challenges she has faced is that most white students use the New International Version of the Bible while she and Jude are alone in using the King James Version or the New King James Version.

Jewel said that in churches like hers the pastors "talk about things that CSF does not really touch on, such as preaching against sin and obtaining the Holy Ghost."[10] Of course, many white pastors do preach against sin, and there are white Pentecostals who also emphasize the Holy Spirit. But from her perspective, these differences are related to differing ethnic backgrounds.

This leads into one place where I think CSF has been most successful in fostering intercultural ministry. Students such as Nick, Faith, Jude, and Jewel have not just sat in a crowd and listened, but they have had the opportunity to share and speak. From the beginning I did not think the best way to reach college students was for me to preach to them for thirty minutes. We always work to include time for discussion. We are very clear that, as Nick observed, all opinions are welcome.

When we are having a discussion, there is rarely agreement in the room. Some of us may be more skeptical of charismatic experiences and speaking in tongues, but students such as Faith and Jude have experienced those things. Because our group is small and welcoming, hearing these things from students who clearly have a strong faith is eye-opening. It is one thing to hear about Pentecostals from a third party who is an observer or scholar; it is another to hear Pentecostals themselves share their experiences and faith.

Strategies for the Future

Clearly I do not write as a disinterested observer. I love college students, CSF, and Penn State. In many ways, I think CSF has done a good job of creating an organization that is not just welcoming to people of all ethnicities but also gives them a safe place to share and opportunities to lead. The experiences of Nick, Brianna, Kevin, Faith, Jewel, and Jude demonstrate this. At the same time, I recognize we could always do better.

Mission Trips, Service Trips, or Any Kind of Trip

Each spring we take a group of students off-campus to serve for a week in disaster relief or in an urban setting. We have also provided mission trips out of the country. Not only do students gain new experiences, but also they have the chance to work under local men and women of a variety of different ethnicities and backgrounds.

I already mentioned my experience going to the Dominican Republic and learning from Henry, a Dominican.[11] One year we went to Miami and volunteered with the Miami Rescue Mission and spent the week working with the homeless. We learned from and were led by an amazing Latina named Bianca.[12] A few years after this we went to Washington, DC, to work with the Center for Student Missions (CSM).[13] In a whirlwind week in the nation's capital, volunteering at soup kitchens and after-school programs, we served under wonderful, mostly African American, workers. Those are the sorts of experiences and memories that university students get when they go off campus.

Getting the students to a place where they can hear from adults such as Henry and Bianca, people who are faithful in Jesus and who look nothing like me and nothing like them, is a key component on the path to intercultural community. This can be a mission trip, or simply a weekend trip to visit the home church of a student. Worshiping together with people different from us can break down barriers and educate.

Interfaith and Intercultural Activities

Campus ministry can also provide students with interfaith activities, which may be intercultural as well. Such activities promote the vital skill of respectful listening to those who are different from us. For example, last fall on campus the Muslim Student Association (MSA) put together an Interfaith Dinner. I was on a panel with a Jewish and a Muslim leader.[14] We each had the opportunity to talk about our respective faiths and share why interfaith dialogue is important.

The event was heavily attended by both Muslim and Christian students. It was an amazing opportunity to hear from people of different religions in a friendly format. When people who might not normally talk to one another are in the same room to listen and learn, beautiful things can happen. We can still disagree, but without listening and understanding we quickly slip into fear.

Examples of fear and misunderstanding are not hard to find. A recent poll found that 30 percent of primary voters supported bombing Agrabah, apparently not realizing it is a fictional place from the Disney movie *Aladdin*.[15] A popular podcast recently hosted a discussion on whether certain terrorist organizations are valid interpretations of Islam.[16] The two panelists who said yes were both white Christians, while it was two non-U.S. Muslims who argued for no. How would I feel if someone wanted to know about Christianity and asked an atheist or a Muslim? Too often we find ourselves talking about other people rather than listening to them.

More and more often people are coming together to talk and listen. Universities are already diverse places, so it is fantastic to see them taking the lead in providing an atmosphere of friendly dialogue. Whether we are talking to someone of a different religion or ethnicity, or any other type of diversity, the key to learning is to shut our own mouths and listen.

Admittedly, as I have worked on this chapter I have felt somewhat hypocritical. Here I am, a white male, giving my thoughts on intercultural ministry on campus and saying we ought to listen more—and I am the one doing all the talking (I mean writing)! I pray the reader will not hold this hypocrisy against me. In working on this chapter, I have been challenged to shut my mouth (or turn off my computer) and spend more time listening. We all need to listen more, but especially those of us who, as members of the majority, possess the privilege that expects others to listen when we talk.

Involving Diverse Students in Leadership

At Penn State Berks we have had diversity on our leadership team over the years. I have many memories of sitting in rooms with college students and hearing diverse students, both leaders and other members, share their understanding of Scripture. Other than continuing to work to have diversity in leadership, what else can we do?

For me, a big part may be stepping back. Rather than facilitating the meeting with discussion in mind, I need to go even further and allow the facilitation and planning to be done by the students. When a diverse group of students do the planning, it will be truly and authentically intercultural.

Along with that, I need to give away my platform more often and open it up to local pastors and guest speakers who are not white—and not male. It will benefit the students for me to invite people who do not look like me, preach like me, or lead like me to share their insights on faith. If I truly care about creating an intercultural ministry that will benefit the lives of the students, then I need to add actions to my words by stepping aside so others can stand up and bring beautiful words filled with the Holy Spirit.

Hope for the Future

I see hope for a strong future of intercultural ministry on campus. Students and campus ministers alike are more aware of the need to listen to all voices. Our CSF ministry had our annual spring break trip. Included among the fifteen students who went were Koreans, Puerto Ricans, Dominicans, African Americans, and whites. We had many conversations about our different church experiences and the way we look at the world. I believe such a team, learning from one another and working together, is the future of not just campus ministry but of the church universal. My prayer is that the students and I can work toward creating a strong intercultural community at Penn State Berks, just as other ministries across the world do the same.

Here is where I stop talking (and typing) and open myself to listen to what my sisters and brothers of all races, cultures, and backgrounds have to say.

Notes

1. For more about the Evangelical Congregational Church, see http://www.eccenter.com/.

2. The story of this transition is told in George Marsden, *The Soul of the American University* (Oxford: Oxford University Press, 1994).

3. A helpful article on some of the history of campus ministry is Tony W. Cauthon and Camilla Jones, "A Description of Traditional and Contemporary Campus Ministries," *The College of Student Affairs Journal* 23, no. 2 (Spring 2004): 158–72. Also helpful is a simple perusal of any organization's Wikipedia page or homepage. I recognize that campus ministry takes other forms; I will focus my writing on the parachurch organizations I am most familiar with.

4. Email correspondence, January 18, 2016.

5. Email correspondence, August 12, 2015.

6. Email correspondence August 8, 2015.

7. Enrollment by race/ethnicity from fall 2015 which, by my calculations, puts all Penn State campuses together at about 70 percent white. Accessed October 27, 2016, http://budget.psu.edu/factbook/StudentDynamic/MinorityEnrolbyEthnicicity ByAdvisor.aspx?YearCode=2015&FBPlusIndc=N.

8. Facebook correspondence, July 13, 2015.

9. Email correspondence, January 19, 2016.

10. Face to face conversation, January 25, 2016.

11. This trip was organized by Adventures in Mission (https://www.adventures.org/).

12. Miami Rescue Mission (http://www.miamirescuemission.com/).

13. Center for Student Missions (http://www.csm.org/).

14. The Jewish representative was from a local synagogue, and the Muslim representative was from the Council of American-Islamic Relations (CAIR) in Philadelphia.

15. Tessa Berenson, "A Lot of Americans Support Bombing the Fictional Country from *Aladdin*," *Time*, December 18, 2015, accessed October 23, 2016, http://time.com/4155228/amiercans-bomb-aladdin-agrabah/.

16. "Unbelievable? Is ISIS Islamic?," November 21, 2015, accessed October 27, 2016, http://www.premierchristianradio.com/Shows/Saturday/Unbelievable/ Episodes/Unbelievable-Is-ISIS-Islamic-Jeremiah-J-Johnston-Craig-Evans-Inayat-Bunglawala-Adnan-Rashid.

CHAPTER 15

The Kin-dom Coming in the Joyful Worship of the God of All People

Rev. Karen Hernández-Granzen

Since I was conceived in the womb of my mother, Margarita, the Holy Spirit was preparing me for intercultural ministry. I am a Nuyorican, a Puerto Rican born and raised in New York City. I am multiracial and multicultural, proud of my heritage as a child born of Puerto Rican parents. I am a descendant of the natives of Puerto Rico (Tainos), the white European Spaniards who conquered Puerto Rico, and the black Africans who were forced to be slaves. I have been an urbanite all my life, having lived or worked in New York City, Los Angeles, San Francisco, Chicago, and Trenton, New Jersey.

In 1994, when I was in the midst of studying for my ordination exams at McCormick Theological Seminary in Chicago, a colleague sent me the congregational information form (CIF) for a church seeking a pastor. I bowed my head with tears flowing as I read the CIF from Westminster Presbyterian Church in Trenton. Even before meeting the congregation, I sensed in my heart and spirit that God was calling me to Westminster. The following quote from the CIF revealed Westminster's commitment to become a multiracial, multicultural worshiping congregation.

> We are a "vintage" congregation of people, many of us born and raised in Trenton . . . a predominantly white congregation, a small band of disciples who still believe that Presbyterians

belong in the city. . . . We know that we are not the same community that existed when most of us lived in the neighborhood
and were not church "commuters" as we are today. We are
aware that we can never be what "was" and that the church we
hope to grow will be of a mixed complexion which reflects the
"now" of our church neighborhood.

It has been more than twenty-one years since I was installed as
the pastor of Westminster. At that momentous event, I was honored to have Rev. Dr. Justo Gonzalez, my professor and mentor,
preach. Although he was preaching to an urban congregation within the Presbyterian Church (USA), his sermon challenged and continues to challenge every mainline or nondenominational homogeneous congregation, be it white, black, Latino, or Asian:

> [W]hile the encounter with many peoples and cultures is intel-
> lectually and emotionally enriching, it is also painful, and
> many people feel justified to resent it. . . . [W]e must confess
> that we are all tempted to privilege our own people, our own
> tribe, our own language, our own nation.
>
> I submit to you that this will be one of the most difficult
> aspects of Christian ministry in this country in the decades to
> come. And yet, faithfulness requires that we continually put
> forth the vision of John, of "a great multitude that no one
> could count, from every nation, from all tribes and peoples
> and languages" (Rev. 7:9), whom God also loves.[1]

Rev. Dr. Gonzalez preached this sermon so that Westminster
would not continue our transformation process naïvely. Over the
years we have learned that radical transformation takes *kairos*
(God's time) and *chronos* (chronological time), genuine compassion, open and ongoing communication, and *mucho* patience.
Westminster's congregational transformation from an all-white,

vintage congregation into a congregation that embraces all of God's people has been and continues to be a long, at times arduous, and ongoing process.

By God's grace and faithfulness, Westminster has truly become an intercultural worshiping community. Westminster was a 100 percent homogeneous congregation on the verge of closing, but now by the grace of God, our membership reflects the mixed complexion of our neighborhood. As of December 31, 2015, our membership of 120 people was comprised of 41 percent European Americans, 47 percent African Americans, 11 percent Hispanic/ Latinos/as, and 1 percent biracial. Every Sunday our joy-filled worship services embrace our children's leadership, as well as traditional, contemporary, multicultural, multilingual, and multimedia worship resources. At the end of the worship service, we share the peace in four languages within a unifying circle as we glimpse the image of God in one another's faces.

As I share excerpts of Westminster's story of transformation, I will focus not on simply objective facts, but on the *historic*, those stories that have informed our present and future identity. Our congregation's mantra is "We've Come This Far by Faith Leaning on God and Each Other." Therefore, my primary goal is to acknowledge God's faithful and guiding presence, as I share the stories of the cloud of witnesses who have gone before us.

A Presbyterian Church (USA) Transformational Story

Changing Demographics

When Westminster began its transformation into an intercultural congregation in the 1980s, the PC(USA) defined that process as a redevelopment process, a radical redirection of its ministry in light of changes in needs or circumstances among its membership, the community to be served, or both. Redevelopment is a very challenging process. It is considered more difficult than starting a new church, because present and future ministries can be stifled by those who say, "But this is the way we've always done it."

The exodus of the white/Anglo community from the city to the suburbs has been occurring for decades throughout all of the cities in our nation, and documented by our denomination in the early 1950s. In 1945 there were twelve Presbyterian churches in Trenton; in 2016 there were only three. Of those three remaining churches, Westminster is currently the only congregation that is fully incarnating the broadest meaning of being an intercultural ministry.

As early as March 23, 1952, the Presbytery of New Brunswick called a joint strategy meeting to discuss the results of a survey revealing the demographic changes in Trenton with all of the trustees and elders of all the city churches. Twelve years later, in 1964, the presbytery's urban work committee invited all active officers to participate in a discussion of "The Church in the Changing City." New Brunswick Presbytery continues to believe that Presbyterians belong in the city, yet even today continues struggling to create an effective urban ministry strategy.

At a Westminster congregational meeting in 1965 the pastor expressed the following:

> We must face realistically the fact that our church neighborhood is changing rapidly in a racial way. This is evident as you walk the streets and as you see the boys and girls going to and from school. We dare not close our eyes to this fact nor our doors to these people in our neighborhood. Christ has called us to minister to all.

Our denomination's resource on redevelopment reveals that churches which experience change and decline often follow the stages of personal grief related to loss: the emotions of denial, anger, guilt, blaming, and finally acceptance. Our denomination also has witnessed that often the first pastor who fully opens the eyes of a congregation in order to help it meet the changing needs of its community becomes a scapegoat, because most congregations would rather avoid facing the challenge. Westminster chose to deal directly with change in the demographics of their community. We opened our doors to the mission at our doorstep.

Implementing Change

Even before Westminster's former pastor, Rev. Dana Livesay, and leaders knew about the PC(USA)'s "Five Dynamic Forces of Congregational Redevelopment," published in the early 1980s, Westminster was implementing them. On October 18, 1987, Rev. Livesay implemented one of the five dynamic forces, "Coming to Terms with the Past, Present, and Future." At that time he presented to Westminster's governing board the following list of possible alternatives, as a response to the realities of declining membership and dwindling resources in the wake of suburban flight:

- continue ministry as usual to present membership;
- reach out to the community and become more integrated;
- continue ministry to present members, but at the same time become a home for a new church development that would reach out to the community but be a completely separate church;
- merge with another church and remain within our building;
- close the church;
- close the church and become the home of a new church development;
- choose the first option and seek to merge with another church and use their building.

It was a major awakening and challenge to Westminster that things could not remain the way that they were. Yet, even at the risk of losing more members, Westminster chose the second option—to embrace its community by being open to radically changing the racial-ethnic composition of its congregational and pastoral leadership.

Rev. Livesay also implemented a second dynamic force, "Re-entering the Community," through faith-based community organizing. Westminster reentered its racially changed community through active involvement in the Interfaith Organizing Committee (IOC). IOC staff facilitated a process to enable church members to build community among themselves. The church later reached out to the neighborhood by participating in listening campaigns through house meetings.

Innovative ministry models, such as The Shared Ministry Experiment led by Rev. Patti Daley, Rev. Dr. Jacqueline Lewis, Rev. John Nelson, and the Trenton Presbyterian Cluster of Churches' Trenton Youth Connection (TYC) ministry, also helped Westminster to clarify God's vision for ministry. Westminster members realized that in order to reveal our commitment to ministering to our diverse community, our congregation would have to call a racial-ethnic pastor. In 1992, Rev. Dr. Jacqueline Lewis became the first racial-ethnic pastor. I followed Rev. Dr. Lewis in 1995.

After gathering helpful suggestions from the congregation, the governing body of Westminster Presbyterian Church at its congregational meeting on March 10, 1996, unanimously voted to adopt the following mission and vision statements.

MISSION STATEMENT
A House of Prayer and Praise for People of All Nations

VISION STATEMENT
As a part of the Body of Christ we are a multiracial, multicultural, and multigenerational congregation where
■ the Word of God is central
■ spiritual growth is nurtured
■ loving, compassionate fellowship is fostered

- traditional and contemporary styles of worship are embraced.
- As Ambassadors of "God's kin-dom"* we are in partnership with the community and other neighborhood churches to seek the welfare of the city through providing
  - ❖ programs and advocacy for social and racial justice
  - ❖ a safe haven and educational opportunities for children, youth, and their families
  - ❖ recovery programs which nurture health and wholeness.

*God's family

This mission statement was inspired by the affirmation in Genesis that we are all created equally in God's image, Pentecost's declaration that the body of Christ is called to be united by the Holy Spirit in the midst of its rich diversity, and Revelation's images of the city of God where all tribes, nations, peoples, and languages will worship God. Westminster again affirmed that this is not without challenges, but the congregation and its leaders believe that this is where God continues to challenge us as Presbyterians who believe that we are called to "abide in" and "seek the welfare of the city."

In 1998, during our centennial anniversary year, the various events, celebrations, and the publication of our Centennial History Book also helped Westminster come to terms with its past, present, and future. In November 2000, Westminster became the first official Radical Redirection Ministry of the New Brunswick Presbytery. One of the most memorable events in our church history occurred in September 2006 when Westminster, along with four other churches, received PC(USA)'s Multicultural Network's First Prize award for our "Multicultural Church Story."

Although Westminster can no longer give financially to our denomination to the extent that we have in the past, we share our God-given gifts and wisdom by leading workshops and providing worship leadership. Our staff and leaders share the wisdom that we have gathered with other churches and leaders who are considering transforming into a intercultural worshiping community and/or reentering their communities by providing programs for children and youth.

Challenges to Creating Intercultural Churches

Creating intercultural congregations has many challenges. I have witnessed to my dismay how the suburbs have helped perpetuate so-called separate-but-equal worshiping communities of suburban whites and people of color in the inner cities. Many white congregations that have remained in the city have remained separate from neighborhood churches that are comprised of people of color. I find it disturbing that many Christians, whites and people of color alike, are not convicted by the fact that despite Martin Luther King's prophetic critique proclaimed more than fifty years ago, Sunday morning continues to be the most segregated time in our society, and the church the most segregated institution.

C. S. Lewis, in *The Great Divorce*, described a vision of hell as a place where people move continually away from one another because they cannot get along. They choose instead to abandon their houses and entire blocks and neighborhoods and to build new houses at the periphery of hell, thereby creating an ever-expanding vacant center.[2] The founder of CrossRoads Ministries, the Rev. Joseph Barndt, says that Lewis's description of hell could be a "description of white flight from the city after WWII and the emergence of suburbs in the United States"[3]

Barndt's *Dismantling Racism* remains a valuable resource for our discussion on intercultural ministry. It reminds us that we can't talk about intercultural churches without first talking about racism, and in order to engage truly in introspection and intergroup dialogue, it is essential to use language that doesn't attack or produce defensiveness. Barndt analyzes the dehumanizing effects racism has on all of us—"people of color and white people alike—

indoctrinated and socialized in such a way as to be made into 'prisoners of racism.'"[4] He writes, "white people, too, live in a 'racial ghetto.' Although we may have built the walls ourselves, the resulting isolation and its effects are equally harmful. . . . Our communities are sterile, homogenous places of look-alike, dress-alike, act-alike conformity."[5] Thus, by addressing racism and its isolating effect on all people, we achieve liberation for all God's family.

Lewis's image of hell certainly comes to mind when I think of mainline urban European American churches that have not enthusiastically welcomed the "mission at their doorstep" when their neighborhood racial-ethnic demographic composition changed. Instead, many respond to declining church membership by joining the "white flight" to the suburbs, abandoning church buildings, and leaving behind God's beloved communities.

A thesis project written by my husband, Rev. Dr. Michael Granzen, provides substantial evidence of the "conspiracy of silence" that exists in the church in regard to open and sincere discussion of issues about race.[6] Robert Terry, an analyst and educator on racism and racial justice, puts it succinctly: "To be white in America is not to have to think about it,"[7] and I would add, not to have to talk about it. Barndt asserts that European American congregations have become complacent and comfortable in their "white ghettoized churches in white ghettoized neighborhoods," no longer questioning whether this situation is a scandal to the gospel.[8] I believe intercultural ministries are the beloved community that Martin Luther King Jr. envisioned and proclaimed.

Instead of being scandalized by how some racially exclusive churches contradict our witness to God's gift of unity, the tendency is to rationalize the existence of these churches by stating, "This is just human nature," or by quoting church growth experts who claim that homogeneous communities are the most effective strategy for optimal church growth, or by clinging to the notion that being a good steward of God's resources means investing primarily in new church developments and redevelopments that are racially specific because their "successful" growth potential is much greater and the church is guaranteed a greater outcome from their investment. Mainline European American Christians have explicitly or implicitly expected Native Americans, African Americans, Hispanic Americans, and Asian Americans to leave their cultures at the door of the sanctuary as they enter a Eurocentric-style worship service and thereby experience "cultural circumcision."[9]

We must become aware of the fact that culture has a dictatorial power that influences our thoughts and behavior by creating unconscious, built-in blinders that become hidden and unspoken assumptions.[10] For instance, there is a hidden and unstated assumption prevalent in the dominant culture of the United States: that "white/Anglo" is not an ethnic group. Minority cultural groups are called ethnic, thereby implying that they are different from the norm because of their race and culture, the norm being the culture of the white/Anglo. Church historian and theologian Catherine Gonzalez observes that this unspoken assumption denies the fact that the white/Anglo worship style is influenced and controlled by their culture. Denying this reality prevents "the unraveling of cultural processes," and thus the white/Anglo worship style becomes superior and the norm.[11]

The other hidden and unspoken assumption is that minority cultures have a uniformity that doesn't exist. For instance, the term "Hispanic American" denies the differences that exist among Hispanics from the Caribbean and Central and South America.[12] And the label "Asian American" obscures the diversity of ethnicities, nationalities, languages, dialects, religions, and cultures encompassed by the numerous countries and ethnic groups of the vast continent of Asia.

Due to the complex, dictatorial power of culture, we all must cling to faith that the Holy Spirit is continually taking our conscious and unconscious conformity to the oppressive elements of this world and transforming it by renewing our minds (Romans 12:2). We can choose to engage in the renewing process of our minds by exposing ourselves to Scripture. Justo Gonzalez's "grammar for reading the Bible in Spanish" suggests that we read Scripture in the vocative voice: "The purpose of scripture is not so much to interpret it as to allow it to interpret us and our situation."[13]

Transforming into an Intercultural Worshiping Community Takes *Chronos* and *Kairos*

Realizing Westminster's God-given mission and vision to become an intercultural congregation by moving from a Eurocentric to an intercultural style of worship has required the delicate embrace of contemporary and traditional styles of worship. During our thirty-plus years of transformation we have had periodic "worship wars" and other conflicts. Westminster has accepted that, given our diversity, conflicts are a given. We cannot be conflict averse. When I became the pastor, I asked the congregation to adopt two norms in order to deal with conflicts in a healthy way: "care-fronting," that is, caring enough about relationships so that conflicts are never avoided but rather dealt with in loving truth telling,[14] and the Latino idiom *hablar sin pelos en la boca,* which literally means "speak without hair in your mouth"; the metaphor means do not swallow your voice. Westminster created many opportunities for Euro-American members to give up their privilege to speak in order to humbly listen to their new multiracial neighbors.

Frederick Buechner has said, "The place God calls you to is the place where your deep gladness and the world's deep hunger meet."[15] That quote resonates with me after each of Westminster's several citywide events, where hundreds of children and families are loved and served. I find myself saying, "I am joyfully exhausted." And the joy makes the exhaustion worthwhile because I know I am fulfilling God's call and because I know I am meeting a deep hunger in the community which is my world.

I truly believe that Westminster and I have embraced our God-given call to become an intercultural missional congregation with a passion and dedication to seeking the *shalom* of the city. Despite our relatively small size and limited resources, God has equipped us to be a cutting-edge leader in urban ministry in the PC(USA) and beyond. Through our seventy-five plus, church nonprofit and private cooperation partnerships, we are actively and effectively engaged in addressing several of our nation's most challenging issues: (1) low-quality public school education, (2) mass incarceration, (3) reentry ministries with returning citizens and their families, (4) via the Bethany House of Hospitality, reaching out to young adults who feel disenfranchised by the traditional church but want to serve the city of Trenton, and (5) assisting immigrants to acquire English proficiency and to secure gainful employment.

I believe that the Holy Spirit has been orchestrating Westminster's transformation process into an intercultural beloved community of God. We have witnessed the Holy Spirit's presence when Euro-American members no longer feel comfortable worshiping in an all-white, Eurocentric church, and when people of color overcome their internalized oppression and are empowered to share their diverse gifts in worship with integrity and joy.[16]

Urban centers need not become forever damned to segregation and isolation; because of their multiracial and multicultural diversity, they are forever blessed! And I heard a loud voice from the throne saying, 'See, the home of God is among mortals. God will dwell with them; they will be God's peoples'" (Revelation 21:3).[17]

Intercultural ministry is challenging, but it can also be enriching and transforming for white people and people of color. According to Paul F. Knitter, cities provide the "sacred space" whereby, as John S. Dunne wrote, "cultures can know and touch each other as never before, persons can be aware as never before of what was from the beginning always real: their common humanity and the many manifestations of the one ultimate mystery."[18]

Notes

1. Justo L. Gonzalez, "A Tale of Two Scrolls," sermon preached at the installation service of Karen Hernandez-Granzen in Trenton, New Jersey, 1995, in Karen Hernandez-Granzen, "Multiculturalism or Cultural Circumcision?," *Renewing the Vision: Reformed Faith for the Twenty-first Century*, ed. Cynthia M. Campbell (Louisville, KY: Geneva Press, 2000), 209.

2. C. S. Lewis, *The Great Divorce* (New York: Macmillan, 1946).

3. Joseph Barndt, *Dismantling Racism: The Continuing Challenge to White America* (Minneapolis: Augsburg, 1991), 54.

4. Ibid., 6–7.

5. Ibid., 110.

6. Michael A. Granzen, "Breaking through the Plate Glass Window: A Study on Race and Religion in Elizabeth, New Jersey" (DMin thesis, Princeton Theological Seminary, 1998).

7. Robert Terry, "The Negative Impact on White Values," in *Impacts of Racism on White Americans*, ed. Benjamin P. Bowser and Raymond Hunt (Newbury Park, CA: Sage Publications, 1981), 120.

8. Barndt, *Dismantling Racism*, 140.

9. Hernandez-Granzen, "Multiculturalism or Cultural Circumcision?," 204–5.

10. Edward T. Hall, *Beyond Culture* (New York: Doubleday, Anchor Books, 1976).

11. Catherine G. González, "The Diversity with Which We Begin," *Reformed Theology and Worship* (Spring 1987), 71.

12. González, "The Diversity with Which We Begin."

13. Justo L. González, *Mañana: Christian Theology from a Hispanic Perspective* (Nashville: Abingdon, 1990), 86.

14. David Augsburger, *Caring Enough to Confront: How to Understand and Express Your Deepest Feelings Toward Others* (Ventura, CA: Regal Books, 1981).

15. Frederick Buechner, *Wishful Thinking: A Theological ABC* (San Francisco: HarperOne, 1993), 119.

16. Hernandez-Granzen, "Multiculturalism or Cultural Circumcision?," 209–10.

17. *The New Testament and Psalms: An Inclusive Version*, ed. Victor Roland Gold et al. (New York and Oxford: Oxford University Press, 1995).

18. Paul F. Knitter, *No Other Name? A Critical Survey of Christian Attitudes Toward the World Religions* (Maryknoll, NY: Orbis Books, 1985), 211. John S. Dunne was a priest, theologian, and long-time professor at the University of Notre Dame.

Conclusion

Rev. Dr. Jann Aldredge-Clanton and
Rev. Dr. Grace Ji-Sun Kim

The challenges of intercultural ministry are great, but the possibilities are greater through the power of Divine Love. Transformation
comes through claiming the prophetic call of the gospel.
Intercultural churches grow from radically inclusive love.
Resurrection Sundays can become everyday realities. These and
other hopeful messages ring out in *Intercultural Ministry*.

Founded on the theology of people of all cultures created equally in the divine image (Genesis 1:27), intercultural faith communities give equal value to people of all cultures so that they can share
power and empower others. Contributors to this book illuminate
other biblical and theological imperatives for intercultural ministry:

■ Mark 11:17 reveals Jesus' vision of a house of prayer for people
of all nations;
■ Acts 2 shows that from the beginning the church was intercultural, multilingual, and egalitarian;
■ Galatians 3:28 presents the ideal of inclusive Christian communities inclusive in culture and gender;
■ Revelation 7:9 provides an end goal for building intercultural
communities with people of all cultures gathered together as equals.

The honest stories and reflections in this book reveal formidable
challenges to building intercultural churches and ministries. White
supremacy, white privilege, and racism pervade our theological,
educational, economic, and other systems. Even when congregations are multiracial, they too often privilege white concerns and

European styles of worship and ministry that discount people of color. Tensions arise when people in the dominant culture resist learning awareness of their privilege through honest conversations about racism. Past and current discrimination and violence from injustices create trauma that hinders the development of intercultural communities. Also, many people who have been hurt by the injustices perpetuated in churches have become skeptical of any kind of organized religion.

In addition to these underlying challenges, many churches face overt resistance to bringing diverse cultures together in community. People are often unwilling to leave the comfort zones of their traditional styles of worship. They may pride themselves on having a racially diverse congregation but oppose culturally diverse music and preaching styles and resist welcoming people with different theologies and political ideologies. To belong to these superficially diverse congregations, people from non-dominant groups have to abandon their individual cultures. Socializing mainly with people of one's own race and culture presents another challenge to building intercultural communities. And then there is the practical challenge of money. Financing intercultural churches and ministries can be daunting because they don't fit the societal norm; thus they may have difficulty attracting enough people who can contribute financially. Pressure often comes from denominational leaders to maintain homogenous communities because of the belief that they maximize church growth.

Contributors to *Intercultural Ministry* provide insightful strategies to overcome obstacles and to build intercultural churches.

1. Confess the sins of racism and white supremacy as we confess other sins.

2. Practice radical welcome of all to lead the world in the work of reconciliation.

3. Address power structures in communities and restructure them so that all cultures represented have equal power.

4. Encourage honest, open conversations about past and current injustices, giving equal value to all voices.

5. Create safe and compassionate communities where people who have suffered the trauma of racism can find healing.

6. Nurture an atmosphere of unconditional love and acceptance.

7. Read and interpret Scripture through the lens of those on the margins.

8. Create space for multiple truths to be engaged and understood.

9. Develop an inclusive leadership team with people of diverse races and cultures sharing equal power, and engage in consensus-based decision making.

10. Address the intersectionality of racism, sexism, classism, heterosexism, and other injustices in order to build communities that are fully inclusive and just.

11. Use language and imagery inclusive in gender and race.

12. Balance culturally diverse styles of music, preaching, and other worship elements and diverse organizational styles.

13. Market to attract people of diverse races and cultures.

14. Engage in faith-based community organizing, advocacy for social and racial justice, and ministries with communities outside the church.

What are the future possibilities of intercultural churches and ministries? Contributors to *Intercultural Ministry* responded to this question with expressions of hope flowing from their experiences in the process of building intercultural communities with the Holy Spirit's transforming power. The possibilities for intercultural churches are great because they are God's ideal as expressed in Scripture. The future of intercultural ministry lies in our willingness to claim our prophetic calling to make reality the gospel vision of radically inclusive love and justice. Those in the dominant culture find freedom from the chains of power and privilege, and those who are marginalized find freedom from the chains of oppression through the liberating power of the Resurrected One.

About the Contributors

Rev. Peter Ahn is founder and lead pastor of Metro Community Church in Englewood, New Jersey, a vibrant, multiethnic congregation. He is president of Zimele USA, which seeks to confront the root causes of poverty in South America. He received his MDiv from Fuller Theological Seminary and is ordained with the Evangelical Covenant Church.

Rev. Dr. Jann Aldredge-Clanton is a feminist theologian and teacher who serves as cochair of the intercultural Equity for Women in the Church Community, adjunct professor at Richland College, and council member of Christian Feminism Today. She is the author of numerous books, including *She Lives! Sophia Wisdom Works in the World* and *Earth Transformed with Music! Inclusive Songs for Worship*.

Rev. Dr. Brad R. Braxton is the founding senior pastor of The Open Church in Baltimore, Maryland, an intercultural congregation committed to social justice activism and interfaith collaboration. He holds a PhD in New Testament studies from Emory University, a master's degree in theology from the University of Oxford, where he was a Rhodes Scholar, and a BA in religious studies from the University of Virginia.

Rev. Dr. Amy Butler serves as senior minister of the historic Riverside Church in New York City. She earned a bachelor of theology from the International Baptist Seminary in Rüschlikon, Switzerland, and the DMin in preaching from Wesley Theological Seminary. A regular columnist for the Associated Baptist Press, she blogs at www.talkwiththepreacher.org.

Rev. Dr. Curtiss Paul DeYoung is executive director of Community Renewal Society (CRS). DeYoung has served as Professor of Reconciliation Studies at Bethel University in St. Paul, Minnesota. He is author and editor of ten books on reconciliation, multiracial congregations, racism, and cultural diversity, including *Coming Together in the Twenty-first Century* (Judson Press, 2009).

Rev. Brandon Green is an associate pastor at River City Community Church and co-director of River City Community Development Center located on the west side of Chicago. Brandon has his master's degree in Christian formation from

North Park Theological Seminary, blogs regularly, and has written for *Christianity Today*.

Rev. Karen Hernández-Granzen has served as pastor of Westminster Presbyterian Church of Trenton, New Jersey, for more than twenty-one years. She earned a Master of Divinity from McCormick Theological Seminary and was a Presbyterian Churches (USA) delegate to the Jubilee World Council of Churches in 1998, in Zimbabwe.

Rev. David Hershey serves as campus minister at Penn State University-Berks. He earned his MDiv and MA in Church History/Historical Theology from Lincoln Christian Seminary. He is ordained in the Christian Church (Church of Christ) tradition and is a commissioned missionary with the Evangelical Congregational Church.

Rev. Dr. Daniel Hill is author of *10:10: Life to the Fullest* and *White Awake*. He is founding and senior pastor of River City Community Church, located in the Humboldt Park neighborhood of Chicago. Daniel has a bachelor's degree in business, a master's in theology, and the DMin from Northern Baptist Theological Seminary.

Angie Hong is a music therapist, worship leader, and liturgical curator concentrating on the intersection of worship and reconciliation. She serves as Creative Director for Willow Creek Church's Chicago campus. She holds degrees in piano and music therapy from the University of Georgia, and leads worship at conferences locally and nationally.

Rev. Dr. Grace Ji-Sun Kim received her PhD from the University of Toronto and is an associate professor of theology at Earlham School of Religion. She is the author or editor of ten books, most recently, *Embracing the Other* (2015) and *Contemplations from the Heart* (2014). She is on the American Academy of Religion (AAR)'s board of directors as an At-Large Director. She also serves on the AAR's Program Committee and has served on the Research Grants Jury Committee. She is an ordained minister of Word and Sacrament within the PC(USA).

Rev. Emily McGinley is founding pastor of Urban Village Church (Hyde Park | Woodlawn), a racially, theologically, and socioeconomically diverse faith community rooted in the United Methodist tradition and located on the south side of Chicago. She is ordained in the Presbyterian Church (USA).

Rev. Katie Mulligan has served as a congregational pastor in Mt. Laurel, New Jersey, and as a youth and young adult pastor for three churches in and around Trenton, New Jersey. Among her publications is "A Ministry of Discomfort" in *From Each Brave Eye: Reflections on the Arts, Ministry, and Holy Imagination.* She is a graduate of Princeton Theological Seminary and ordained in the Presbyterian Church (USA).

Bishop Karen Oliveto is the first openly lesbian bishop of The United Methodist Church. She was senior pastor of the 11,000-member Glide Memorial United Methodist Church and was adjunct professor of United Methodist Studies at Pacific School of Religion. She has a PhD in Religion and Society from Drew University, and is coauthor of *Talking about Homosexuality: A Congregational Resource* (Pilgrim Press, 2005).

Rev. Carlos Ruiz, originally from Oaxaca, Mexico, has lived in the United States for eighteen years. He holds the MDiv from North Park Theological Seminary and a master's in clinical psychology from Wheaton College Graduate School. He currently works bivocationally as a clinical psychotherapist and as a pastor and church planter.

Rev. Sheila Sholes-Ross currently serves as senior pastor of First Baptist Church of Pittsfield, Massachusetts. Ordained by the American Baptist Churches USA, she has a Master of Divinity from James Walker Hood Theological Seminary, as well as master's degrees in public health and administration and supervision. She cochairs the ecumenical, intercultural nonprofit Equity for Women in the Church Community.

Rev. Christine A. Smith has served as senior pastor of Covenant Baptist Church, Euclid, Ohio, since 2006. She is author of *Beyond the Stained Glass Ceiling: Equipping and Encouraging Female Pastors* (Judson Press, 2013). She earned her MDiv from the Interdenominational Theological Center, Morehouse School of Religion. Founder of Women Together in Ministry of Greater Cleveland, she writes a weekly blog, *Shepastor*.